THE LOST THREAD

31 51

Populism As Creative destruction.

ALSO AVAILABLE FROM BLOOMSBURY

THE LOST THREAD

The Democracy of Modern Fiction

BY JACQUES RANCIÈRE

Translated by Steven Corcoran

Bloomsbury Academic
An imprint of Bloomsbury Publishing Plc

B L O O M S B U R Y
LONDON · OXFORD · NEW YORK · NEW DELHI · SYDNEY

Bloomsbury Academic
An imprint of Bloomsbury Publishing Plc

50 Bedford Square	1385 Broadway
London	New York
WC1B 3DP	NY 10018
UK	USA

www.bloomsbury.com

BLOOMSBURY and the Diana logo are trademarks of Bloomsbury Publishing Plc

First published in French as
Le Fil perdu. Essais sur la fiction moderne
Paris, La Fabrique Éditions, © Jacques Rancière 2014

First published in English 2017
© Copyright to the English edition Bloomsbury Publishing Plc 2017

Steven Corcoran has asserted his right under the Copyright, Designs and Patents Act,
1988, to be identified as Translator of this work.

British Library Cataloguing-in-Publication Data
A catalogue record for this book is available from the British Library.

ISBN:	HB:	9781472596017
	PB:	9781350025684
	ePDF:	9781472596031
	ePub:	9781472596024

Library of Congress Cataloging-in-Publication Data
Names: Ranciere, Jacques, author.
Title: The lost thread : the democracy of modern fiction / by Jacques Ranciere ;
translated by Steven Corcoran.
Other titles: Fil perdu. English
Description: New York : Bloomsbury, 2016. | Includes bibliographical references and
index.
Identifiers: LCCN 2016017994 (print) | LCCN 2016034469 (ebook) | ISBN
9781472596017 (hardback) | ISBN 9781472596031 (epdf) | ISBN 9781472596024
(epub)
Subjects: LCSH: Fiction–History and criticism.
Classification: LCC PN3331 .R2613 2016 (print) | LCC PN3331 (ebook) | DDC
809.3/034–dc23
LC record available at https://lccn.loc.gov/2016017994

Typeset by Fakenham Prepress Solutions, Fakenham, Norfolk NR21 8NN
Printed and bound in India

CONTENTS

HISTORICIZING DISSENSUS: TRANSLATOR'S INTRODUCTION

Jacques Rancière's *The Lost Thread* explores the much-studied advent of modern fiction in the nineteenth century, its emergence from the hierarchy of genres and subjects characterizing pre-modern fiction. But while much ink has been spilt about this in twentieth-century modernist and structuralist discourse, Rancière argues that the essential anti-representational stakes of this transformation of literary fiction have been missed. What occurred was nothing less than a revolution in the ontology of fiction, the consistency and ramifications of which have gone largely misunderstood. *The Lost Thread* is thus an attempt to historicize what he sees this revolution as being about, that is, its specific dissensus, or untimeliness. In this, it continues the work he did in *Aisthesis,* which bears on the texture and logic of what he calls the aesthetic regime of art.

For Aristotle, something could be counted among the arts if it was endowed with a story of significance, possessing a beginning, a middle and an end; if it had an organic structure in which all the details were subordinated to the work's overall perfection. But the new world of sensation and affect forced a rethink of this rationality. Gustave Flaubert's literary realism marked a point of rupture with representational logic, as literature began to appear as a sensible mode in its own right: fiction came to manifest a growing disproportion between the preparatives for action and the unfolding of its action, going so far as to abolish any regulated succession from the immateriality of thought to the materiality of action. Flaubert's novels, like those of Joseph Conrad and Virginia Woolf after him, undid the beautiful proportions that, since Aristotle, had defined fiction as a structure of rationality: the middle no longer appeared as a point of passage between a beginning and an end, but more as a milieu without meaning; details seemed to detach themselves from their internal organization; gaps opened up between effects and causes, depriving the tale of intelligibility through its temporal development; fiction lost its vertebral column, ceasing to be a body that stood by itself.

The new fiction came to be 'cluttered' with a twofold excess. It became inundated with what the rationality of representationalist poetics had necessarily excluded. If fiction necessarily entailed the interconnected causal unfolding of events in accordance with the rules of verisimilitude, then what it excluded, as Aristotle claimed, is the *kath' hekaston,* or empirical succession of historical facts as they simply occur, without rhyme or reason, one after the other. This story about fiction's manifest signs of change is an old one. If Rancière gives it a new twist, it is not in the manner of a Roland Barthes, by providing another interpretation of its non-manifest workings as part of a governing narrative structure. Instead, he takes into account what structuralist and modernist accounts of this transformation necessarily miss, namely the other side of this excess inundating the new fiction. To the succession of random events that simply happen one after the other corresponds the people who, unable to think at the level of the whole in order to distinguish themselves through grand actions or refined feelings, cannot do otherwise than simply have things happen to them. *The Lost Thread* turns precisely on the singular ways in which the new fiction reinscribes this outside – of things and people encountered in the randomness of life – within itself.

Conservative critics at the time deplored this cluttering of the space of fiction once reserved exclusively for the thought and refinement of the elite by insubordinate details and the prosaic concerns of ordinary everyday individuals. A century later Roland Barthes would interpret this disproportion between the immobilities of description and the dynamics of action in new literature as an attempt to recover the lost verisimilitude of Aristotelian representationalist poetics: he conceptualized this excess of superfluous details hindering narrative action as an '*effet de réel*', or reality effect. Fiction is cast here not as a structure of rationality but instead as an imaginary realm somewhere between being and nothingness. But it is productive: the specificity of this fiction, as Barthes has it, consisted in an attempt to reify (market) reality, at naturalizing history in a capitalist society in which the old fixed modes and genres and hierarchies of subjects that defined pre-modern fiction no longer held. Rancière takes issue with both the conservative critic and the progressive intellectual, whose positions are by no means opposed; for the real issue, which forms the central task of this book, is to grasp this 'overcrowding' of the space of pure fiction modern fiction as a dissensus with, and as a process of what I will call a 'creative destruction' of, the representational regime of fiction. It is nothing less than the forging of a new rationality of fiction itself – under what conditions and how this is done are the subject matter of this book.

Historicizing this dissensus of modern fiction – grasping it as a transformative event in the very structure of rationality of fiction itself – means grasping the new subjects and the new objects, the new problems and paradoxes, that it brings forth. But doing this means dismissing a twofold obfuscation of this event: on the one hand, the conservative critic's view of the 'cluttering' of the space of fiction as a mere series of random events without backbone, a simple pile of facts. The critic dubs this 'invasion' of a space and time, now too cluttered by the 'prosaic' concerns of ordinary individuals to allow the distinguished elites the room to develop their grand actions and unfold their fine feelings, as follows: it is democracy in literature. But understanding this nomination pejoratively, he is nostalgic for the eternal time of the old order and fails to see the consistency of the revolution in the ontology of fiction underway. As Rancière reminds us, realist fiction in the manner of Flaubert or Conrad is for this critic simply a monster without order, a random succession of empirical facts without causal linkages, of details that signal an equality without rationality. It is viewed as a simple destruction of the old order, a fruitless ruination to be cast aside in the restoration of the proper representational order of fiction. As suggested above, the progressive intellectual, on the other hand, views this destruction, this proliferation of descriptive excess ruining representation, as a sort of stopgap to a loss of order. It is an attempt at reinventing representational effects by inundating the narrative structure with excessive description of a paradoxical usefulness: descriptions of objects, for example, whose sheer purposelessness indicate the unconditional realist of their being *there*. The usefulness of the figures and images go the new fiction, then, is precisely to signal the eternity of the new (bourgeois) reality, its historical permanence. For this intellectual, realist fiction thus maintains verisimilitude, against the background of a simultaneously destructive dimension, since it works to recode mores, demystify taboos, eradicate inherited psychic structures, and so on. However, its unidimensional and closed temporality – as is implied in its forging of a 'reality effect' – means it is unable to make the creative leap outside representation toward authentic artistic modernity, understood as a signifying process possessing its own autonomous logic. Barthes subscribes to the modernist vision of a historical event that breaks through History, separating out a time before and a time after. And this modernism links together a historical process of political emancipation and a historical process of the autonomization of artistic practices. Understanding representation as simple figuration or resemblance, for him the task, at once political and literary, was thus to sweep away all parasitic images of the real and bring about the purification of narrative structure. As Rancière magnificently shows, despite their differences, Barthes's position thereby rejoins that of the conservative critic. For both encounter the 'scandal' of this excess that they insist on keeping out. Both thus necessarily maintain an emphasis, in their own ways, on the fictional time of cause–effect linkages, of action, which, as Rancière argues, is the very core of representational poetics.

Where Barbey d'Aurevilly and other critics could see only unstructured, irrational excess, and Barthes the ideological naturalization of historical process, Rancière unfolds for us the slow transformation of fiction in its break from the representational regime. The creations of modern fiction, rightly seen, have a consistency and rationality that is founded upon the ruin of the structure of rationality of the old fiction and its organic model of action. This process of destruction is an immanent one: it is not merely a negative term to be discarded or an intermediary step on the way to genuine creation but simultaneously a positive means of construction, an activity replete with its own temporality and logic – a creative destruction.

As diagnosed by Rancière, this rupture entails a full-blown revolution in the ontology of fiction. If new fiction is 'democracy in literature', *pace* Aurevilly it is because of the *effects of equality* it is able to generate. This democratic revolution, as Ranciere argues throughout, can only occur on the proviso that the ontology of action and the idea of thought that goes along with it – and which are hierarchical in essence – are shattered and new bodies and subjects able to emerge. It thus unfolds not through manifestos, but, as he points out, through dispersed attempts at reworking the relation between fiction and its outside, that is, at reorganizing the relation between two ways of linking events: on the one hand, fiction as a temporal development obeying a sequence of cause–effect relations subordinated to an overall end; and, on the other, the pile of data, or succession of historical facts as they occur. What occurs in this reorganization is that the split between the fictional plot and its outside becomes internal to fiction itself, through a work of thought and practices of writing that transform this outside by producing specific fractures with the regime of representation. What Rancière gives us to see through the genealogy of modern fiction, and the surprising collection of novelists, poets and playwrights that he summons here, is the consistency and the ramified conse-quences of this revolution.

Flaubert, as Ranciere argues in the opening essay, was the first to see clearly that the real of old fiction had been under-mined. The time of action, which formed the core of the representational regime, and its hierarchy of life forms, which had 'defined the space of fiction and commanded its organic unity', had simultaneously given way to a space of sensible coexistence of all individuals, things and situations – what Rancière elsewhere calls an aesthetic democratism. Flaubert's solution as to how to reconfigure the rationality of fiction under these conditions, he knows, cannot come through the series of concepts that once defined the fictional whole. It must come in and through the *kath' hekaston,* on the condition, however, that its status is altered. In Flaubert, the random succession of empirical facts is no longer the outside of poetic rationality, but becomes the time itself of a 'democracy of sensible coexist-ences', 'a chain of sensible events that weaves thoughts and wills' themselves, that which constitutes the contingent interlacings informing individual experiences. The whole is now in the *kath'* *hekaston,* in the detail; or rather, it is in the power of linking, in the *impersonal* breath that holds together sensible events and has them produce 'those singular condensations that are called love or desire' (34). It is this impersonal Life of micro-events that enables the modern fiction writer to provide fiction with a new texture, one corresponding to the equality of all subject matter, which is to say the negation of any relation between a determinate genre and a determinate form of life.

For the question, Rancière argues, is not about the ontological status of the real – it is not to know, as he puts it *pace* Barthes, whether 'the real really is real' – but instead is about the *texture* of this real. And the texture of the real is not about analysis, but rather about the life lived by those who inhabit it. This texture is one that undoes the hierarchies of the old fiction and thereby operates, as Rancière so convincingly shows, an effect of equality. This new real is a 'de-hierarchized' one. As we read in *Un Coeur simple*, from now on, it is the preserve of any woman from the lower classes to be able reach the vertiginous heights of passion formerly reserved for the elite, with a force of passion that rends holes in the routine of existence. But the effect of Flaubert's new absolute style is that the status of the thoughts, feelings and wills that unfold in the narrative also changes. Everything under the writer's pen is treated with the same care. The character can therefore no longer be a subject that is the source and master of its thoughts and feelings. Instead, it becomes a simple point of conjunction between, on the one hand, the 'rain of sensible events' that unconsciously inform thoughts and feelings – which thus seem reduced to the status of epiphenomena – and the plot logic of social identities and causal relations, which become merely dream-like but never-theless still obtain. In the Flaubertian novel, these two times of cause–effect linkages and of the *kath' hekaston* thus become interwoven in a new logic. In this logic the status of narrative action is altered, since the novelistic action moves forward only through the impulses received from random coming together of sensations, affects, memories, etc. But the forward movement is nonetheless interpretable by the novel's characters in represen-tational terms (in *Madame Bovary* Emma interprets the love she feels/is made to feel for Rodolphe as *her* love for him). So, Rancière argues, Flaubert at once cements the ruin of the old fiction and, by having the time of the *kath' hekaston* work in conjunction with that of verisimilitude, makes a concession to it.

With the novels of Conrad, which Rancière explores in the book's second essay, the interlinking of these two times of new fiction gets radicalized. Conrad takes further this logic of the 'luminous halo' of sensible micro-events, in and through which thoughts, wills and dreams are produced. He abolishes the logic of verisimilitude and its category of probability. What is interesting for him, Rancière argues, is no longer to be able to anticipate the probability of what happens in its effects. The moment is no longer a moment in a time of succession leading to a possible social end; instead it becomes the moment in which the time of regulated succession is blown apart altogether.

Conrad's description of Lord Jim's leap from the *Patna* belongs to the order not of the possible but of the real – it sets in motion a chain of events that tears Jim from the ordinary time of succession, and brings to light that which stood for Conrad as the sole certitude: our being inevitably caught in the unmasterability of the real. The leap attests, among other things, to the split in any moment: a moment can be a link in a verisimilar plot, or it can be the point at which an entirely inconceivable and real rupture occurs in one's existence and which, by suspending the false solidity of verisimilitude, reveals the lie of the plot. What Rancière calls the 'clarity of the detail' is the impossibility of reconstructing the act's conceivability. Ultimately, Conrad constructs a time-space in which it is not that the real is reached so much as the idea that any notion of the real is a fiction. But this is not to say that all is dream, but instead that all is real; it means that the real and dream are caught in a fundamental indistinction.

Virginia Woolf's novels, as Rancière details in the third essay, then come to deepen the problematic – one which cuts through any categorization of writers into realist or modernist (indeed, for Rancière, the history of modern fiction in literature *is* the history of the realist novel). Woolf radicalizes the ways in which the luminous halo is able to suspend the tyranny of the plot, her novels being about exploring differing ways in which this can happen and the tension between them. She makes clear the other limit of realist fiction: it can never dissolve purely into a musical phrasing of the luminous halo of sensible micro-events, precisely because this impersonal Life has no proper form of its own. Thus, while the ontology of realist fiction is monist, its practice is necessarily dialectical: it consists in staging the 'tension between the grand lyricism of impersonal Life and the arrangements of the plot' (67). Woolf's major novels, *Mrs Dalloway* in particular, represent a singular achievement in the way she presents the dialectic that structures fiction by dividing it.

This first part devoted to exploring the tensions of the realist novel takes up half the book. Brief as the above remarks are, perhaps we can nonetheless venture to claim that Rancière gives us fresh insight into Fredric Jameson's musings on the hybrid character of the notion of realism. As Jameson notes, realism presents both an epistemological claim (for knowledge or truth) and an aesthetic ideal of beauty or satisfaction. However, for Jameson these dimensions remain incommensurable, whereby joining them together has fatal consequences for both: the claim to social truth or knowledge leads us to ideology; while the claim to an ideal of beauty or aesthetic satisfaction traps us in 'outdated styles or mere decoration (if not distraction)'.[1] Yet this is clearly only the case if realism is deemed to have 'a vested interest, an ontological stake, in the solidity of social reality, on the resistance of bourgeois society to history and to change'.[2] But, for Rancière, the aesthetics of the realist novel

– the clarity of details, the absolute style that translates the 'very life of the whole, the impersonal breath that holds together the sensible events', etc. – manifest precisely the contrary of the immediate emotional gratification and lack of intellectual effort that characterize kitsch, nor do they have anything to do with the ornamental devices of epidiectic oratory. At the same time, Rancière demonstrates that the suspensive capacity of the grand impersonal Life is about revealing the lie of the plot, and thus about transmitting situations 'at the limit of the recountable'. What is thus transmitted in them is the paradoxically contingent state of whatever passes as reality. In response to Jameson, it might thus be said that these two dimensions – of truth and aesthetic style – far from being incommensurable, actually imply one another. Moreover, the idea of the politics of fiction that can and must be drawn from modern fiction cannot be said to simply lapse into ideology; the specific politics of fiction concerns the ways in which it constructs its own logic(s) of equality. Literature is not political by attempting to reify the so-called (politico-economic) real. As Rancière has argued in numerous works, it has its own politics, and it has them because it constructs its own logics of equality: logics that stand in dynamic, irreducible tension with one another; logics that, in this tension, are irreducible to any construction of a given reality.

Part Two of the book, The Republic of the Poets, explores the developments of modern fiction in poetry, with separate essays on John Keats and Charles Baudelaire. In the first, Rancière discusses the politics of Keats's poetic work, which he sees as developing a metapolitics that is fundamentally irreducible to the usual split between contextless, apolitical beauty on the one hand, and the promotion of a concrete political determination on the other. Keats approaches the question of the 'justice of the poem' through that of the 'availability of works'. This latter question shifts considerations of the politics of the poem. For Keats, the question is one of the quality of their availability. Why? Because for him poetry is not essentially as a way of writing but instead as a way of reading and of transforming what one has read into a way of *living*. Poetic disinterest is the work of an imagination that does not attempt to configure the common fabric of life so as to ensnare its reader; instead, it ceaselessly takes from and gives to this fabric in such a way as to address itself to another intelligence. Keats understands that this can only be done by viewing the democracy of co-presences horizontally, and thus in opposition to the vertical Christian interpretation of it, which reserves a special place for the poet, alone able to see and show to others the divinity of creation in each singular manifestation of life. A thorough-going equality demands the exercise of the paradoxical (in)activity of 'diligent indolence': the idea of an equality of fragments, sensations or signs, equally animated by the power of the whole, is not something that can just be discovered among ordinary beings on the road; instead, it requires a practice of weaving the web of poetry that, traced bit by bit, extends to infinity the power of a singular arrangement of these sensations or these signs. Reciprocally, all individuals have this ability to weave a poem on their own account, attaching to all the infinity of different leaves that others have made available. From this, Rancière is able to shed light on what he sees as Keats's unique version of a certain poetic vision of the community, qua community of individuals who participate in a sensible equality that is 'experienced in the singularity of encounters and of communications, and not in the universality of laws'.

The essay on Charles Baudelaire likewise sets the Baudelairian reverie of the 'infinite taste of the Republic' against the vast set of transformations that affect the poetic paradigm in his time. On the one hand, knowledge has become divorced from the finite world required for the organic model of action; the world is now too vast for the calculation of probable causes and effects. Its scene extends beyond the finite world required for the logic of mastered action. On the other, impersonal life, as a power that that traverses bodies, exceeds their limits and disorganizes the very relation of thought to its effects. As such the agent of the action no longer has a temporality that coincides with the source of its action. It is this context against which the transformations of the poetic form and the creations of *reverie* are to be grasped. Rancière's interpretation of reverie thus differs from Benjamin's, which sees it as a poetic transcription of the devastated experience of modernity in the era of High Capitalism. This enables him to show that this 'infinite taste' is not merely the passing fad that once saw Baudelaire actively side with the 1848 revolts; instead, it is the category of a consistent aesthetic politics. Nor is reverie a withdrawal into oneself due to disappointment experienced with the external world; more crucially, it is a mode of thought that challenges the boundary that the organic model imposed between 'inner' reality, in which thought decides, and 'outer' reality, in which it produces its effects.

Finally, the last essay, on the theatre of thoughts, examines what happens in the theatre chiefly of Maurice Maeterlinck and Georg Büchner within this configuration, in which life turns the stage into the place of a new dramaturgy, a dramaturgy of coexistence. The forms of this coexistence involve a separation of the powers of thought, speech and action. As three powers of the theatre, they must therefore receive a new articulation: the breath of the great impersonal Life demands the development of a new rationality of theatre. It demands that an image of the thought of theatre be forged that is in rupture with both the Platonic and Aristotelian ones. Rancière's argument is that the new law of theatre is precisely that thought acts only inasmuch as it is an unmasterable territory. Thought in this new configuration becomes a twofold excess: first, over acts, which are unable to follow the rhythm of the succession of thoughts; and second, over itself, as their provenance is something the mind 'cannot master, determine the justice of, or fix by itself the means of realization'. Büchner endeavours to radicalize the status of thought, as a law of the outside. Here we see a complete undoing of the opposition between thought qua unity of the multiple and the isolated succession of facts that we started with. Thought itself becomes subject to line of infinite fracturing, ruining both the Aristotelian and Platonic models. It becomes a disordered succession of 'facts of thought'.

What all these essays thus contribute to doing is to mapping the historicity of the revolution of modern fiction and its dissensus with the regime of representation. Rancière is careful to avoid attributing this revolution any global cause. Its development, to be grasped, must be thought of immanently: every transformation effected within it is describable in terms of how it undoes, or suspends, distinctions constitutive of the former fictional rationality, each time in a new, singular fashion. Every new destruction of this old paradigm is a sort of repeat affirmation of this revolution and is in turn inseparable from a new phrasing of connections, a new landscape mapped, and a novel way of inventing solutions or aporias – in short, from its own creative activity. If modern fiction cannot be reduced to a deformed expression of any such cause, then, it is because its specificity, as Rancière so brilliantly shows, rather lies in the various ways in which it suspends cause–effect logic and explores the moment as a point of potential rupture.

To emphasize a global cause is to allow the progressive intellectual to do what has apparently been reserved for him: to think at the level of the whole, in the name of a revolutionary humanity still impeded in its development by the strictures of ideology. Now, this is what could be called a sort of plot lie. The 'falseness' of the knot of relations it implies – between the revolutionary people championed by the intellectual, the knowledge of the intellectual, and the oppressive order of power – was something Rancière first encountered during the turbulent events known as May 1968. These events were fundamental in showing Rancière that between the intellectual bearing an aim of socio-political transformation, who brings to workers the knowledge of their oppressed condition from the outside, and the oppressive order of power there is not an opposition but a complicity. They both operate according to categories that imply the masses' incompetence – structural or natural – concerning politics. It was this lie concerning the image of the people's incompetence that May '68 overturned, since during it ordinary citizens arose to verify, against the presupposition of its incompetence, that which had been denied them, namely the basic equality of anyone and everyone. And they did so by producing forms of argumentation, of knowledge and of experience that manifested a common competence, a common power of intelligence.

What Rancière has strived to show in many ways, ever since he first sought to grasp the fracturing of categorial divisions that had sustained the power/knowledge nexus, was the nature of the presupposition of inequality sustaining this nexus and its utter contingency. This fracturing effected by the people showed indeed that the science of the intellectual (or the schoolmaster's pedagogy) is not based in any science of the real at all. Instead of having a position grounded in a knowledge of reality, what is occupied is the real of a position. This means that hierarchical positions of the sort are grounded only in their own exercise, only in the repeated creation of their conditions of existence. At the heart of progressist logic, therefore, another time opens up, which is the time of a continual reopening of the gap separating those who know from those who don't, basically through the telling of the oppressed about their condition – and first and foremost, through getting them to understand their incompetence or inability to understand. But political dissensus shows that emancipation is not achieved by being in tow to intellectuals with an understanding of the whole, but instead through a movement that is subtracted from hierarchical divisions and in doing so reveals the common power of the equality of intelligences.

If I recall this part of Rancière's trajectory, it is because *The Lost Thread* traces a similar knot in the modernist and structuralist reception of modern fiction. It is a reception that cuts too quickly through the web of transformations affecting poetic rationality (its rearticulation of the two ways of linking events we have rapidly traced) toward the unique cause to which all literary phenomena can be reduced. In so doing, it fails to take into account the population of fiction, a population whose emergence is inseparable from the singular effects of equality this literature operates.

Modernist and structural reception is thus also way off target when it claims to discern beneath the surface of the modern text a historical narrative (one with capitalism, for example, as its centre) with a concrete agent (the bourgeoisie); when it claims to see in Flaubert's sentences a bourgeois strategy to thing-ify human relations to the detriment of the open future of action, of proletarian advance. In projecting this vision of the people and the radical emancipation of humanity, it fails to see those effective appearances of the people, those egalitarian forms of disidentification of one's gaze from one's body, of one's speech from one's social destination. This disidentification is not describable in terms of the positivity of the social field. Similarly, a specific politics of fiction is made possible only through the logics of equality specific to fiction itself, logics that tear it from the representational regime. Or, to put it another way, just as politics for Rancière involves blurring the boundaries between those deemed destined to politics and those regarded as inhabiting the social, through a demonstrative speech that departicularizes political universality, so too can fiction have a politics, properly speaking, when it is freed from representational conventions through a work of writing that anonymizes the real.

Modern fiction, Rancière shows, is both a literary, poetic and dramaturgical phenomenon, as well as being a symptom of the quality of social and political life. For if there is a historical point of anchorage for modern fiction, it resides precisely the forms of intellectual and political emancipation enacted by those that social destination would appear to have condemned to the endless repetition of bare life. Disincorporating themselves from that social plot, ordinary workers and women displayed an unprecedented capacity, a capacity of everyone and anyone. This anonymous power, which appeared only in singular, local suspensions of the social plot, is key to the revolution of modern fiction. Writers of new fiction would appropriate it for themselves, turning it into the impersonal power of writing that phrases the luminous halo. Yet, the nineteenth-century movements of emancipation will have been its absent centre.

FOREWORD

'There isn't a book in it; there isn't that thing, that creation, that work of art of a book that, organized and developed, marches toward its dénouement via paths that are the secret and genius of the author.' This is how, in 1869, a French critic judged a work that had been recently published. Thirty years later, an English newspaper would address the same sort of reproach to another new book: 'To tell the honest truth, it drags. The paragraphs, for one thing, are far too long. They sometimes wander on for pages. The book wanders on in the same way. It is full of atmosphere, full of the magic of the East, but it lacks vertebration. The want of backbone paralyses the book.'[1]

Thus discredited were two novels that posterity will ordain masterworks of modern literature, Flaubert's *L'Éducation senti-mentale* and Conrad's *Lord Jim*. If I recall these judgements, it is not to validate the received idea about novelty disrupting conventional criticism. I intend, on the contrary, to take seriously what this sort of criticism tells us: books that for us are exemplary were initially non-books, erratic accounts, monsters lacking backbone. During the times of *L'Éducation sentimentale* and *Lord Jim* something happened to fiction. It lost the order and proportions by which its excellence was judged. This was the view held by those critics who perceived Flaubert to be wandering aimlessly like the idle youth that is his paradoxical hero, and Conrad to be losing his way ever more in pursuing the flight of his anti-hero towards the most distant islands. This same sentiment is one that these innovators themselves also experienced. Rereading the second part of *Madame Bovary*, Flaubert finds the work's disproportion troubling: does the length of the 'prologue', which develops the 'picturesque, grotesque and psychological preparatives' of the action, not require the novel to extend to over 75,000 pages if he is to 'establish a close to equal proportion between the Adventures and the Thoughts'?[2] But if proportion presents the novelist with a problem, this is precisely because the writing of this 'prologue' has erased, line after line, the very gap between the immateriality of thought and the materiality of action, between the time of 'preparatives' and that of 'adventures'. For Conrad, the indistinction between the action and its prologue, thought and adventure, is an acquired thing. Moreover, he has no hesitation in positively asserting the vagabondage for which others reproach him. To a colleague who complained about all the *sideshows* that interrupt the story of *Lord Jim*, he replied simply that the *main show* itself, the story of the ship with its hundreds of pilgrims abandoned in cowardice, 'is not particularly interesting – or engaging'. Hence the necessity, he says, of introducing into the sketch 'a good many people I've met – or at least seen for a moment – and several things overheard about the world'.[3] But by dismissing the most universally accepted principles for constructing stories, the author of *Lord Jim* reopened a fundamental question: what makes a literary fiction different from a simple account of things and people encountered in the happenstance of life? And he had to confront the reply commonly accepted since Aristotle: what separates fiction from ordinary life is to have a beginning, a middle and an end. Conrad resolved half of the problem by beginning his tale (*récit*) with the middle and by making this time of the middle no longer a median point but the sensible cloth out of which the 'thoughts' and the 'adventures' are made. But he could not shirk the other obligation, which is to complete the tale with its ending. And he had to confer this ending to a *deus ex machina*, to an adventurer who appears from nowhere to provoke the gunshot that is alone able to stop Jim's roving. Conrad justified this purely factual ending to his editor: enough is known about Jim's psychology at this stage of the story, he said, to allow one to stick to the bald facts.[4] But the problem is more radical: passing from 'psychology' to 'facts' means breaking with the very principle of new fiction, which is no longer to separate action from its 'preparation'; it means being unfaithful to this sensible fabric, which renders adventures and thoughts indistinct. New fiction is without end. The books it produces must have an ending, but it is perhaps doomed never to be the good ending.

The essays collected here attempt to think through some of the transformations and some of the paradoxes that found modern fiction on the destruction of what seemed – and still often seems – to found all fiction: the backbone that makes it a body standing by itself; the internal organization (*ordonnance*) whereby the perfection of the whole subordinates the details; the chain of causes and effects that ensures the story's intelligibility through its temporal development. This revolution was not achieved through manifestos, but instead via shifts in writing practices. Sometimes these shifts were deliberate attempts, but sometimes also surprises even for those undertaking them. So it is that this revolution will be treated here through singular cases: solutions found by a writer to alter the nature of events comprising a fiction, to give it new characters, other temporal sequences, another form of reality or necessity; thus, with Virginia Woolf, we have the attempt to recount the story of an uninhabited house via the purely material events affecting its walls and objects; or, with Flaubert, the way, again, in which a chain of sensations produces the event of a hand surrendering itself; or, with Conrad, of a body leaping into a boat. But this revolution will also be broached through the problems raised for readers and critics by fiction's new proportions or dispro-portions; this is the case of the disequilibrium between the immobilities of description and the dynamics of action that Roland Barthes interprets through the category of the 'reality effect'. I will try to show that the 'realist' excess of description can be interpreted quite differently, if one takes account of the relation between the population of fiction and the structure of fictional action, and to draw from it a wholly other idea of the relation between the poetics of fiction and its politics.

This relation was most often posited within a problematic of representation. Now, this problematic is doubly reductive. On the one hand, it places fiction on the side of an imaginary to which it contrasts the solid realities of action, and notably of political action. On the other, it explains its structures as the more or less deformed expression of social processes. But, as we have known since Aristotle, fiction is not the invention of imaginary worlds. It is first a structure of rationality: a mode of presentation that renders things, situations or events perceptible and intelligible; a mode of liaison that constructs forms of coexistence, succession and causal linkage between events, and gives to these forms the characters of the possible, the real or the necessary. Now, this twofold operation is required wherever it is a matter of constructing a certain sense of reality and formulating its intelligibility. Political action, which names subjects, identifies situations, links events and deduces possibles or impossibles from them, uses fictions just as novelists or filmmakers do. And likewise for the social sciences, which retain their very possibility from the literary revolution that blurred the ancient opposition between the causal rationality of poetic fiction and the empirical succession of historical facts. True, the social sciences readily forget this when attempting to explain the inventory of fictional schemas on the basis of the reality of social processes. But the price to pay for this forgetting is that they thus explain fiction simply by means of another fiction. Playing this role in the 'political' interpretation of literary schemas is the concept of reification. This sole concept made it possible to reduce the descriptive exuberance of Balzacian novels, the impersonality of Flaubertian style, Baudelairian flanerie, the visual epiphanies of Conrad, of Proust or of Virginia Woolf, Joycean interior monologue, 'modern' formalism and 'postmodern' fragmentation all to a single cause, namely the commodity form that conceals human labour. But reification is by no means the concept of an economic process that would serve as a basis or model for others. It is merely one interpretation of the evolution of modern societies. The origin of this concept can be found in the Schillerian critique of the division of labour. This critique came to be intercepted by counter-revolutionary discourse about the human community that revolutionary abstraction has broken, then became transformed into the romantic opposition between the organic and the mechanical, and the young 'sciences of the spirit' reprised it and communicated it further to the sociology of 'rationalization', prior to Lukacs's identifying it with Marxian commodity fetishism and it becoming the one great fiction that serves as the foundation for all others. The essays gathered here would like to show that this fiction of politics, focused on the becoming-thing of human relations – alienation, reification, spectacle – has not ceased to mask the real political stake, which bears on the very nature of these 'human relations'. An entire progressist tradition has seen in the modern revolutions of fiction a process of fragmentation of the human totality or of dethroning of action in favour of the passivity of things. The following pages encourage us to see in it something else altogether: a destruction of the hierarchical model subjecting parts to the whole and dividing humanity between an elite of active beings and a multitude of passive ones.

I will therefore localize the politics of fiction not in terms of what it represents but in terms of what it operates: the situations that it constructs, the populations that it convokes, the relations of inclusion or exclusion that it institutes, the borders that it traces or effaces between perception and action, between the states of things and the movements of thought; the relations that it establishes or suspends between situations and their meanings, between temporal coexistences or successions and chains of causality. In their principle, none of these operations is proper to literary fiction. And the ritual interrogation into the relations of politics and literature could usefully be replaced by an analysis of paradigms in which facts are presented, events linked up and sense constructed, paradigms that circulate between the various domains of human knowledge and activity. But, from another angle, avowed forms of fiction enable us to perceive the logics behind the presentation of facts and production of their sense that invoking the given in its self-evidence or scientific necessity hides elsewhere. The Aristotelian rules of fiction subtend the principles that realist political action, social science and media communication lay claim to. And, conversely, disturbances of the fictional order make it possible to think through the new relations between words and things, perceptions and acts, repetitions of the past and projections of the future, the sense of the real and the possible, of the necessary and the verisimilar, from which forms of social experience and political subjectivation are woven. This is the perspective from which I will analyse herein the paradoxical forms of novelistic democracy, the singularities of the poetic Republic and the disturbance of relations between thought and action that the theatre reveals on the very stage where it convokes the people of revolutions and that of the *fait divers*.[5]

PART ONE

THE LOST THREAD
OF THE NOVEL

1

Madame Aubain's barometer

In 1968 Roland Barthes wrote a text that was destined to become
canonical: 'The Reality Effect'. The model that guided him, and
that dominated structuralist reflection on fiction at the time,
came from the analysis of stories that the Russian formalists had
carried out in the 1920s. This analysis reduced the imagination
of popular tales to the arrangement of a definite number of
fundamental narrative relations. But the beautiful simplicity of
the model encountered difficulties when it came to dealing with
so-called realist fiction, in which the story is overcharged with
descriptive elements irreducible to narrative functions. Barthes
illustrated the problem with a detail taken from Flaubert's *Un
coeur simple.* At the beginning of the story, the novelist describes
Madame Aubain's house, which serves as the setting of the
action, and he dwells on a detail: 'An old piano supported, under

a barometer, a pyramidal heap of books and boxes.'[1] Plainly, this barometer has no use; it has no function in the story. From the viewpoint of structural analysis, it is a parasitical piece of information that, as Barthes says, using an economic metaphor, 'increases the cost of narrative information'. This denunciation of the superfluous barometer extends a long critical tradition that laments the vain descriptive proliferation of the realist novel. In the *Manifeste surréaliste*, André Breton lashes out at Dostoevsky's minute description of the usurer's room in *Crime and Punishment*. For him, this description consisted merely in 'so many superposed images taken from some stock catalogue'.[2] In the prologue to *Morel's Invention*, Jorge Luis Borges rounds on the French realist and psychological tradition. There are, as he puts it, pages and chapters of Proust that as inventions are unacceptable and to which 'we resign ourselves as to the insipidity and the emptiness of each day'.[3] And to this he contrasts those well-constructed detective novels, which unfold 'odysseys of marvels' that are the logical consequence of a single fictional postulate.

But the structuralist theoretician cannot be satisfied with the modernist humour of making such declarations about realist triviality. If the realist work contravenes the structuralist principle that banishes the superfluous detail, then for its part structural analysis has to account for 'the entire surface of the narrative fabric'.[4] So it has to account for superfluous details, which amounts to showing that they are not superfluous, that they also have a place and a function in the structure. Barthes initially considers descriptive superfluity to be the relic of the ancient tradition of epideictic oratory, in which the object of description supposedly counted for less than the unfolding of brilliant images and metaphors showing the author's virtuosity in being able to satisfy the merely 'aesthetic' pleasure of the listener or reader. He shows its derivation in the famous panoramic description of the town of Rouen that Emma Bovary's extra-conjugal trips occasion. But a barometer is an object of limited aesthetic seduction. This useless accessory must therefore be found another use: its usefulness lies precisely in its being useless. If an element is found in a tale without there being any reason for its presence, it is because this presence is unconditional; it is there simply because it is there. Such is the at once simple and paradoxical logic of the reality effect. The usefulness of the useless detail is to say: I am the real. The real has no need, in being there, to have a reason for being there. On the contrary, it proves its reality by the very fact that it serves no purpose, and therefore that no one had any reason to invent it.

This outright self-evidence is, for Barthes, the modern substitute of verisimilitude, which has provided the norm of the representational order since Aristotle. But it is precisely only a substitute. The realist novelist cannot make the leap from the ancient mimetic order to authentic modernity, that of the signifying process possessing its autonomous logic. But this substitute for a defunct order is itself impressively fecund. It becomes, Barthes tells us, the kernel of a fetishism assuring us 'that the "real" is supposed to be self-sufficient, that it is strong enough to belie any idea of "function", that its "speech-act" has no need to be integrated into a structure and that the *having-been-there* of things is a sufficient principle of speech'.[5] Doubtless today's reader will be amused to see stigmatized this evidence of the 'having-been-there' that the author of *Camera Lucida* was to celebrate twelve years later. The Barthes of 1968 continued to remain close to those Brechtian times in which he dismantled bourgeois 'mythologies' that transformed history into nature. Analysing the reality effect for him was akin to denouncing the way in which a social order is given in the evidence of what is simply there, natural and inviolable. This dismantling concurs with Sartre's analyses on literature: in Flaubert and the writers of his generation, Sartre denounced an obstinacy to thing-ify everything, to petrify everything, in which he saw the strategy of a bourgeoisie threatened by social praxis and eager to escape its condemnation by transforming works, gestures and actions into stone. More broadly, an entire critical tradition of the twentieth century sought to denounce the minute descriptions of the preceding century's realist novel as the product of a bourgeoisie at once cluttered with its objects and keen to affirm the eternity of its world imperilled by the revolt of the oppressed.

It may well be, however, that these analyses miss the core of the problem. I will attempt to show herein that the inflation of description over and against action, which comprises the singularity of the realist novel, is not about the bourgeois world's parading of its wealth in its concern to affirm its perennial existence. No more than it is the triumph of representational logic that so many readily describe. It marks, on the contrary, a rupture with the representational order and with what resides at its core, the hierarchy of action. And this rupture is linked to what stands at the centre of nineteenth-century novelistic plots: the discovery of an unprecedented capacity among common men and women to accede to forms of experience hitherto denied them. Barthes and representatives of the critical tradition ignored this upheaval because their modernist and structuralist presuppositions continued to be too anchored in the representational tradition that they purported to denounce.

We must, to hear this, return to the judgement of disapproval leveled at *L'Éducation sentimentale*. Barbey d'Aurevilly deemed it lacked the organized development of a book: 'M. Flaubert does not understand the novel in this way. He proceeds without plan, pushing along, without any higher preconceived notion, not even suspecting that life, under the diversity and the apparent disorder of its coincidences, has its logical and inflexible laws and its necessary engendering [...] It is a stroll in the insignificant, the vulgar and the abject for the pleasure of walking about in it.'[6] The problem, for Barbey, is not that there are superfluous details, there simply to say 'we are the real'. The problem is that there is *nothing but details.* The novel is missing that which is the very condition of fiction. Fiction has to be a body in which the parts are coordinated under the direction of a centre. This judgement's founding model, one which structures representational poetics more broadly, is clearly identifiable. It is that of the organic totality posited by Plato as posited as the characteristic of living discourse and by Aristotle as the principle of the poetic work. Poetry, said the latter, is not a matter of music, it is not a rhythmic combination of words. It is a matter of fiction. And fiction is a succession of actions linked by necessity or by verisimilitude. This is why fiction is 'more philosophical' than history. For history has only to do with the *kath' hekaston,* with the succession of facts as they arrive, one after another, whereas poetry has to do with the generality of things grasped in their ensemble (*ta katholou*), that is to say, with the succession of events as they *might* occur in accordance with the casual relations of necessity or verisimilitude.[7]

That is precisely what founds, for Barbey, the inferiority of the realist novelist: the one who 'pushes along' by ignoring 'necessary engendering'. It is crucial to gauge the extent of the privilege given to poetic rationality over historical empiricity. In order to be constituted into forms of scientific knowledge, historical and social science had to borrow from poetry the principle that declares the construction of a verisimilar causal sequence more rational than the description of facts 'as they occur'. For fiction is not fantasy as opposed to the rigour of science. Instead, it is what supplies the latter with a model of rationality. And precisely this model is the one threatened by the superfluous presence of barometers or other accessories of the same kind. Far from being a triumph of representational poetics, this invasion of prosaic reality could well be its ruin.

It is also because the poetic distinction between two types of linking events rests on a distinction between two types of humanity. The poem, says Aristotle, is an arrangement of actions. But action is not simply the fact of doing something. This category organizes a hierarchical division of the sensible. According to this division, there are active men who live at the level of the totality, able to conceive grand ends and to seek to accomplish them in contention with other wills and the blows of fortune. And there are men who simply have things happen to them one after the other, able only to live day to day in the mere sphere of reproduction of life's reproduction and whose activities are only ever means to ensuring this reproduction. These latter are called passive or 'mechanical' men, not because they do nothing but because they do nothing other than do, as they are excluded from the order of ends, which is that of action. Such is the political core of representational politics. The good Aristotelian organization of the poem's action rests on this prior division between active men and passive men. The same division applies to the plots of the classical age, when the emotions and passions of souls came, in the France of Louis XIV, to replace the blows of fortune. The verisimilitude lying at the core of representational poetics concerns not only the relation between causes and effects. It also bears on the perceptions and feelings, the thoughts and actions able to be expected from an individual in accordance with his condition.

For those who pass judgement on Flaubert, this articulation of the poetic order with the division of conditions is self-evident. And in all naturalness do they link the disorder of these headless stories to a subversion of social conditions. In reporting on *Madame Bovary,* the critic Armand de Pontmartin gives this reign of the 'detail', which renders all the novel's episodes equally important or equally insignificant with one another, its name. It is, he said, democracy in literature. This democracy is, first, the privilege given to the material outlook and, by the same token, it is the equality of all beings, all things and all situations open to being seen. But if the details of the description are all equally insignificant, this is because they concern people whose lives themselves are insignificant. Literary democracy means too many people, too many characters alike all the others, unworthy therefore of receiving distinction through fiction. This population clutters the story. It leaves no place for the selection of meaningful characters and the harmonious development of a plot. To the contrary, in the novel of aristocratic times space was opened through the stratification of social positions: 'In the novel, such as it was formerly understood, in that novel the delightful model of which *The Princesse de Clèves* has remained, the human character represented by all the superiorities of birth, mind, education and heart, left little place, in the economy of the *récit*, to secondary characters, still less to material objects. This exquisite world looked at little people only through the doors of its carriages and at the countryside only through the windows of its palaces. Whence a large space was open, and admirably filled, for the analysis of feelings, subtler, more complicated, more difficult to unravel in elite souls than among common people'. On the other hand, in the realist school of which *Madame Bovary* is the example, 'all the characters are equal […] The servant boy, the groom, the beggar, the kitchen woman, the apothecary boy, the gravedigger, the vagabond, the dish-washing lady take up an enormous space; naturally the things surrounding them become just as important as they are; they might be distinguished from them by the soul alone, and in this literature, the soul does not exist.'[8]

This critique states bluntly the social basis of the well-constructed beginning and the organic work. A good structural relation of parts to the whole rests on a division between souls of the elite and commoners. Certainly the little people have always had their place in fiction. But it was exactly the subalternate place or inferior genre in which it was permissible for them to amuse the audience by acting and talking as befits people of their kind. It is this distribution of roles that the new fiction destroys. On this point, the frightened critic of democracy misses the crux of the problem. He sticks to the clichés of counter-revolutionary imagery, which view the space formerly structured by branches of great oaks as henceforth smothered by the copse of democratic shrubs. But the ill runs deeper still. The problem is not that vulgar beings saturate with their prosaic concerns the space formerly devoted to the unfolding of refined feelings. Rather, their new passions happen to blur the division itself between souls of gold destined for exquisite feelings and souls of iron doomed to prosaic activities.

Such is the trouble borne in the story cluttered by the famous barometer. *Un coeur simple* is the story of a poor illiterate servant whose monotonous existence is marked by a series of unfortunate passions that hone in on, successively, a lover, a nephew, the daughter of her mistress and, at the end of the road, a parrot. This is the context in which the barometer has its sense. It is not there to attest that the real really is real. For the question is not to know if the real is real. It is about the texture of this real, that is to say, the type of life that the characters live. The barometer probably entered the story without any preconceived intention, there quite simply because the novelist 'saw' it while thinking up the story's setting. But if he saw it this clearly, it is because this prosaic instrument encapsulates an entire sensible world. The needle that indicates variations in atmospheric pressure also symbolizes the immobile existence of those whose horizon is limited to knowing each morning the favourable or unfavourable conditions that the weather will lend to the day's activities. It indicates the separation between those who live the succession of work and days and those who live the temporality of ends. From now on, it happens to mark something else: the relation these obscure existences have with the power of atmospheric elements, the intensities of sun and wind, and the multiplicity of sensible events whose circles expand to infinity. The world of work and days is no longer one of succession and repetition, opposed to the grandeur of action and its ends. It is the great democracy of sensible coexistences that revokes the narrowness of the old order of causal consequences and narrative and social proprieties. *Un coeur simple* testifies to the revolution that occurs when a life commonly doomed to endure the rhythm of days and variations of climate and temperature, assumes the temporality and intensity of an exceptional chain of sensible events. The needle of the useless barometer marks an upheaval in the distribution of capacities of sensible experience in which life doomed to utility is separated from existences destined for the grandeurs of action and passion. The humblest, most nondescript being is henceforth granted the grand intensities of the world: it has the ability to transform the routine of everyday existence into an abyss of passion, whether this passion is directed at a young man or at a stuffed parrot. The purported 'reality effect' is much rather an equality effect. But this equality is not the equivalence of all individuals, objects and sensations under the writer's pen. It is not true that all sensations are equivalent, but it is true that any one of them can trigger for any woman of the lower classes the vertiginous acceleration that opens her to experiencing the depths of passion.

Such is the meaning of this literary democracy. It strikes at the political heart of the principle of verisimilitude by which the proportions of fiction had been governed. From now on, anyone whomsoever can experience any emotion or passion whatsoever. The object of this passion matters little in itself. Felicity in *Un coeur simple* is a model servant, inured to every task and fanatically devoted to serving her mistress. But this fanaticism carries disorder within. Felicity does not serve as she should, in line with the logic of social decorum and fictional verisimilitudes. She serves with an intensity of passion far surpassing her mistress's own capacity for emotion. This intensity is not only useless – it is also dangerous, just as is every sensible capacity that exceeds what is required for daily service. Extreme devotion is close to radical perversion. Some years before *Un coeur simple,* Flaubert's colleagues and friends, Edmond and Jules de Goncourt had published a different servant story, *Germinie Lacerteux,* inspired by their personal experience. Germinie was also a servant fanatically devoted to her mistress. But in the course of the novel it happens that the same passion making of her a model servant could also make her a woman capable of going to the most extreme lengths of physical and moral degradation in order to satisfy her passions and her sexual desires. The angelic Felicity and the monstrous Germinie are two sides of the same coin. Both belong, with Emma Bovary, to the formidable species of those daughters of peasants capable of doing anything to sate their most sensual passions or their most ideal aspirations. This new capacity of anyone at all to live any life at all ruins the model linking the organicity of the story to the separation between active and passive men, elite and vulgar souls. It produces this new real, made of the very destruction of the old 'possible', this real which is no longer a field of operation for the aristocratic heroes of grand actions or exquisite feelings but the interlacing of a multiplicity of individual experiences, the lived fabric of a world in which it is no longer possible to distinguish between the great souls who think, feel, dream and act and individuals locked in the repetition of bare life. Flaubert had no sympathy for political democracy. But the story of Emma, eager to verify in her life the meaning of a few stolen words in books destined for souls of the elites – bliss, passion or intoxication – is akin to attempts made by emancipated workers to reconstruct their daily experience out of the words of the romantic heroes who suffer from not having 'anything to do in society', or those

Potential/Equality –

made by revolutionaries to formulate the new equality in words borrowed from ancient rhetoric or from the evangelical text. It is akin to the audacity of those young dressmakers who the words of Saint-Simonian 'new Christianity' were to move so much that they made themselves the educators of a humanity-to-come, all the while sharing, on occasions, the beds of the young preachers from the polytechnic school. Against a fate of immobility, the story of Emma expresses the multiplicity of these 'silent revolts' that, as Charlotte Brontë puts it, 'ferment in the masses of life which people earth'.[9]

There is no 'reality effect' that stands in as a substitute for old verisimilitude. There is a new texture of the real produced by the transgression of boundaries between forms of life. And this transgression changes the texture of fiction under its twofold aspect as arrangement of events and as relation between worlds. The story of Emma Bovary does not attest, as is always said, to the distance between dream and reality. It testifies to a world in which the makings of one are no longer different to the makings of the other. The real is no longer a space of strategic deployment of thoughts and wills. It is the chain of perceptions and affects that weaves these thoughts and wills themselves. This weaving is what defines the new textures of novelistic episodes. Reactionary critics of the time complained, together with Barbey, that action sequences had been replaced with a series of 'tableaus', or pictures, simply pinned up next to one another. Progressive critics of the following century would readily come to see this reign of immobile images as the expression of capitalist reification. But these 'tableaus' are not images, nor are they immobile. They are differences, displacements and condensations of intensities through which the external world penetrates minds and these minds form their lived world. This blended fabric of perceptions and thoughts, of sensations and acts is what, from now on, will constitute the lives of Zola's proletarians as much as Virginia Woolf's bourgeois ladies, Conrad's adventurers of the Eastern seas or Faulkner's black and petty white folk of the Deep South. But this fabric was first the new music of indistinction between the ordinary and the extraordinary, which seizes within the same tonality the lives of servants in the countryside and those of great ladies of the capital, the music expressing the capacity of anyone at all to experience any form of sensible experience at all.

Barthes's analysis misjudges this political stake because the idea of structure that governs it – and that governs the ideology of artistic modernity more broadly – is itself dependent on the organic model that governed the representational order. It contrasts descriptive excess to an idea of structure as the functional arrangement of causes and effects subordinating the parts to the whole. Structural analysis has to assign a place in the structure to each narrative unit. It thus encounters the same scandal that the champions of representational poetics faced with a fictional fabric made up of 'details' without narrative function in the narrative totality. But the political stake, which was still clear to the former, gets rubbed out in the context of triumphant 'modernism', which imagines it is criticizing the logic of representation where it reprises its most resistant core. Barthes analyses the 'reality effect' from a structuralist viewpoint, one that identifies literary modernity and its political impact with a purification of the narrative structure, sweeping away parasitic images of the 'real'. But literature as a modern form of the art of writing is exactly the contrary. It is the abolition of the border that had delimited the space of fictional purity. What is at stake in this excess is not the opposition between bare singularity and structure. It is the conflict of two divisions of the sensible. This conflict happens to disappear when the functionality of structure is opposed to the superfluous 'detail'. As it also does when the rupture with the representational logic of action is conceived through the concept of reification. This concept places at modernity's core the loss of a totality of lived experience. But this 'totality' was one of a world strictly divided into two worlds of experience without communication. And the democracy of modern fiction works to revoke this division.

However, this does not therefore entail that fictional democracy goes hand-in-hand with political democracy. The equality specific to the new fiction belongs to this redistribution of forms of sensible experience, in which the forms of worker emancipation also participated, as did the multiplicity of rebellions that assailed the traditional hierarchy of forms of life. But it did not for all that express political aspirations for democracy or social emancipation. Sartre sought to discern in the petrifying power of Flaubert's style the nihilist strategy of a bourgeoisie threatened by the development of the proletariat and by worker insurrections. But a far larger contradiction sees the novelistic genre, in the nineteenth century, triumph in accompaniment with the ruin of the model of strategic action. From Balzacian conspirers who fail in all their undertakings to Tolstoyan generals who imagine that they lead battles whose success depends upon a thousand interlacing causes that elude their strategies, including Dostoevsky's Raskolnikov, who conceives the ends of his action rationally but executes them solely as a hallucination in act – the novel of that century did not cease to proclaim the bankruptcy of strategic action, even as it showed us heroes methodically engaged in the conquest of society. Elsewhere I have evoked the strange duplicity of the apparently simply fable *Le rouge et le noir,* which in fact contrasts two forms through which the subversion of social positions is presented to the young ambitious plebeian: as conquest of power or as sharing of a sensible equality.[10] And I have suggested seeing in this individual story a tension that affects the forms of popular revolution and of demonstrations of worker emancipation on a completely different level: the discovery of the capacity of anyone at all to live any sort of experience seems to coincide with a defection of the schema of strategic action of adapting means to ends. This tension lies at the heart of the most resolute undertakings of social transformation. Prior even to linking means of action to demonstrations of knowledge, the new Marxist science identified the revolutionary realization of human essence with the abolition of the separation between means and ends.

It is thus not really by opposing its sensible equality to the ends of action that literary democracy is separated from the other one. The tension between sensible equality, strategic action and the science of society belongs, far more broadly, to the history of modern movements of emancipation. But the new literature also carries out a scission in this very sensible equality, linking transformations of the novel form to the silent, or noisy, rebellions of ordinary men and women searching for another life. The enterprise of Emma Bovary, eager to experience the meaning of a few words read in books not meant for peasants' daughters, testifies to a larger movement of affirming the capacity of the anonymous: workers' sons and peasants' daughters, identified by the occupation of a defined place in the social totality and with the form of life reserved for them in accordance with that position, broke with this identity assignation. They broke with the universe of repetitive and invisible life in order to engage capacities and live forms of life that did not match their identity. These operations of disidentification, which undo 'normal' relations between identities and capacities, were what made possible the literary revolution that destroys the identities and hierarchies of the representational order. But this revolution itself accomplishes a very precise operation with regard to these subversive demonstrations of the power of the anonymous. It separates this power from the agents who put it to work in order to make it its own power, the impersonal power of writing. This appropriation comprises two operations. The first decomposes these manifestations of the capacity of the anonymous into a dust of impersonal sensible micro-events. The second identifies the movement of writing with the respiration of this very sensible fabric.

The first operation may be illustrated by *Madame Bovary*'s most famous episode, in which we are told of the birth of Emma's love for Rodolphe amid the bustle of the country fair. In it, Rodolphe deploys the classical arsenal of words and attitudes likely to seduce a provincial petite bourgeois woman. However it is not this logic of means adapted to the end that ensures his success. Emma's love is born in fact as the modification produced by a chain of sensible events arriving *kath' hekaston,* one after the other, without their aggregation being the effect of any reckoning: the heat of a summer's afternoon, the voices of speakers swirling around in the air, the bellowing of oxen, the bleats of lambs, small rays of gold radiating out all around black pupils, a vanilla and lemon scent, a long plume of dust trailing a stagecoach, the remembrance of a waltz and of longstanding desires swirling like grains of sand in gusts of wind, the final outcome of which is that a hand – hers – surrenders to another hand – the seducer's. Her love is thus born as the effect of a multiplicity of sensible micro-events, carried away in one and the same flow, also made up of words read in books, of images seen on plates, of coloured vignettes decorating missals or keepsakes, of altar scents and of choruses from sentimental ballads.

Novelistic democracy opposes this order of sensible coexistences to the old order of consequences and proprieties. But this democracy comes at a price: the disquieting ability of the anonymous to live other lives than 'their own' is absorbed in the flow of micro-events, which transforms its manifestations into singular crystallizations of the great impersonal Life. If anyone at all can have the refined sentiments previously reserved for 'souls of the elite', it's because these refined feelings are no longer what they were. They are no longer intimate dispositions of individuals but instead chance-ridden condensations of a whirlwind of impersonal sensible events, a 'life of the soul' still unknown: a perpetual movement of an infinity of atoms that are assembled, separated and assembled again within a perpetual vibration. This movement is what gives this new fiction its texture. This movement is what provides the response to critics who denounce this fiction for its inability to subordinate its 'details' to the unity of the whole. The opposition of the poetic *katholou* to the empirical *kath' hekaston* had its time. The whole is now in the details. It is in the common breath, which sweeps along the succession of these events freed from the chains of causality. It is no longer found in the balance of the plot's parts. It resides in the work of writing, in that 'style' that rightly no longer has anything to do with the charms and ornaments of epideictic speech, since it translates the life of the whole, the impersonal breath holding together the sensible events, and it has them produce these singular condensations called desire or love. So fictional democracy puts to work a very specific form of equality: the equality of phrases of which each bears the power of liaison of the whole, the egalitarian power of the common respiration animating the multitude of sensible events.

Sensible equality thus passes over to the side of writing. And the capacity of the character who had embodied it is split into two parts: on the one hand, the individuality of Emma Bovary is a condensation of impersonal events; on the other, it is an identity defined by narrative functions corresponding to social forms of identification: a peasant's daughter, a dweller of a small market town, daughter, mother, spouse and mistress. The character is defined at the intersection of two sensible worlds, that of the impersonal dance of atoms and that of social identities and properties. But this conjunction of two worlds is also the principle of a new hierarchy. The character is separated from the writer by the impossibility of seeing that duality. Emma lags behind the recounting of her story. She can perceive only the interlacing of sensible events weaving 'her' love. She interprets this interlacing in the classic terms of identity and causality as the story of her love for another person. She thus becomes prey to the old narrative and social logic to which the novelist opposes the power of his sentences. The writer sacrifices the character whose subversive egalitarian power he has appropriated to render it as the impersonal power of writing.

But the operation that abandons the character of new fiction to the old representational logic also turns this fiction into a compromise. Flaubert was the first to raise the problem of modern fiction: what system of relations between characters and situations can constitute the fictional work when the old hierarchy of forms of life that defined the space of fiction and commanded its unity is ruined? How are we to reconcile the new world of perceptions and sensations that this ruin liberates with the necessity to construct a whole comprising a beginning, a middle and an end, that is to say also a history of wills and actions leading to successes or else to failures? And he found an answer that became a model for modern fiction: the solution does not exist at the level of the whole. It must come from the *kath' hekaston*: not only at its level but rather through it. Writing that incorporates the new power of sensible equality must exercise a twofold function. By uniting one sentence to another one and one narrative event to another, it must also construct a bridge between the logic of impersonal connections of life and the logic of social identities and causal relations. The new logic of coexisting sensible states and the old logic of linked actions can thus glide imperceptibly over each other. The writer inserts in the interstices of stories about love and money the vibration of the great impersonal equality of sensible events, thus producing the imperceptible deviation, at the level of the sentence, that changes the model of production of narrative action. But the matter can be stated in reverse: the expression of this great equality is only embodied in the vibration of the sentence so as to be better subjugated to the old logic of action: village intrigues, stories of imaginary loves and very real worries about money. The anonymous power of the sentence ends up playing, as regards the old logic of the plot, the same role as Emma's artistic initiatives, by which Charles Bovary is seduced but without understanding the enticement: 'They added something to the pleasure of his senses and to the sweetness of his home. They were like gold dust sprinkled all along the little path of his life'.[11]

2

Marlow's lie

Is this compromise by which the new music of phrases sprinkles with golden sand the old path of the plot not a lie that sacrifices the truth of experience to the demands of bad tailors? It's against the latter that Virginia Woolf publishes the manifesto asserting the full rights of modern fiction.[1] Her text takes the directly opposite view of critics who, sixty years earlier, had denounced Flaubert's 'materialism'. The materialist sin, for them, was to have substituted successions of 'pictures' for the organic order of the story. Woolf inverts the argumentation: the true materialists are the partisans of well-made plots and of parts subordinated to the whole. The novelists who embodied this ideal, Arnold Bennett, John Galsworthy or H. G. Wells, are materialists, she said, because they are only interested in bodies and not in the 'life of the soul'. 'They write of unimportant things […] they spend immense skill and immense industry making the trivial and the transitory appear the true and the enduring.'

But 'so much of the enormous labour of proving the solidity, the likeness to life, of the story is not merely labour thrown away but labour misplaced to the extent of obscuring and blotting out the light of the conception'.[2] The life of the soul does not resemble these well-sculpted wholes. It is made up of an always changeable shower of sensible events. At each moment of each ordinary day 'the mind receives a myriad impressions – trivial, fantastic, evanescent or engraved with the sharpness of steel. From all sides they come, an incessant shower of innumerable atoms; and as they fall, as they shape themselves into the life of Monday or Tuesday, the accent falls differently from of old.' The task of the free writer is thus to 'record the atoms as they fall upon the mind in the order in which they fall', to trace 'the pattern, however disconnected and incoherent in appearance, which each sight or incident scores upon the consciousness'.[3] The hurried reader might ask what the difference is between the 'trivial' and the 'evanescent' of this shower of atoms and the 'trivial' and the 'transitory' to which old-school novelists sought to give a true and enduring aspect. It's an easy answer to provide: the difference lies precisely in the way of treating the insignificant and the ephemeral. 'Materialists' want solidity. And, concerning fiction, the solid is called the verisimilar: the transformation of the shower of atoms into qualities belonging to identities; the integration of incidents into a recognizable schema of causes and effects. 'Materialists' seem constrained 'by some powerful and unscrupulous tyrant who has him in thrall, to provide a plot, to provide comedy, tragedy, love interest, and an air of probability embalming the whole.[4] Woolf thus overturns the Aristotelian opposition: the logic of verisimilitude is an anti-artistic lie. With regard to the great democracy of sensible atoms, the order of things, things 'such as they could be', exercises a tyranny comparable to the Table of Precedence in Whitaker's Almanack, according to which the Archbishop of Canterbury is followed by the Lord High Chancellor, who is himself followed by the Archbishop of York.[5] The truth is in the fall of atoms; it is in the *kath' hekaston*. But this is not the insignificant proceedings of successions and repetitions of daily life; it is the great coexistence, the universal life immanent to each aleatory configuration of atoms. It is not a matter of contrasting the singular with the totality, but instead one mode of existence of the whole with another. And it is naturally a totality of an atmospheric type, a diffuse totality made up of discrete particles which are substituted for the organic model of the whole: 'Life is a luminous halo, a semi-transparent envelope surrounding us from the beginning of consciousness to the end.'[6]

Woolf did not invent the image of this luminous halo. She borrowed it from another English-language writer, Joseph Conrad. At the beginning of *Heart of Darkness*, the narrator in effect indicates what distinguishes Marlow's stories from the ordinary stories of sailors: 'to him the meaning of an episode was not inside like a kernel but outside, enveloping the tale which brought it out only as a glow brings out a haze, in the likeness of one of these misty halos that sometimes are made visible by the spectral illumination of moonshine.'[7] But thus formulated Marlow's poetics might in fact define the revolution Conrad himself undertook in the domain of fiction: it is not in the linkages of the story that the fictional content is to be sought. This content, which one seeks always on the inside, is to be found outside, 'around' the story. The luminous halo is not a diffusion of light from a centre. The central light is there, on the contrary, only to reveal the sensible power of the atmosphere in the midst of which it is plunged. The flame is at the service of the fog, the centre at the service of the periphery. This means that, for this admirer of Flaubert, the luminous halo can no longer be confounded with the gold dust sprinkling the march of the plot. It is the plot that ought to be enveloped in the luminous halo and which has as a task to illuminate it, to illuminate this new fabric of fiction that is the fabric of human experience grasped in its truth.

The sense of the story is in what surrounds it, that is to say, the milieu of meaning, the milieu of actions. And, of course, the milieu of meaning is itself devoid of meaning, the centre of actions is itself inactive – not because nothing happens in it but because what happens in it is no longer conceptualizable or recountable as a succession of necessary or probable actions.

Conrad was the first to give a theoretical status to this tendencial indistinction between the action and its 'preparation', whose artisan Flaubert was astonished to be. He was able to do so, of course, because in the interval separating his stories of seas of the Orient from the Flaubert's stories of provincial mores, the properties of the new fictional fabric had become the elements of a philosophy of life. The abolition of the separation between active humans and passive humans had been incorporated into the equal respiration of the phrases of the new prose. But this equality of phrases, weaving the uniform web of perceptions and actions, of thoughts and adventures, also came to be transformed. It became the philosophical belief in the vanity of thoughts that believe they are freely elaborating their ends and of actions that believe they are following the straight line of their realization. And captain Conrad, returned from the seas and from the mirages of adventures that promise their names and their outlines on maps, himself took up the nihilist belief in that vanity. To a socialist friend concerned with improving the lot of a humanity now known to be condemned to perish from the cold, he affirms both the expressions of that belief in the vanity of human actions and the words that turn it into a vanity itself: 'If you take it to heart it becomes an unendurable tragedy. If you believe in improvement you must weep, for the attained perfection must end in cold, darkness and silence. In a dispassionate view the ardour for reform, improvement for virtue, for knowledge, and even for beauty is only a vain sticking up for appearances as though one were anxious about the cut of one's clothes in a community of blind men. Life knows us not and we do not know life – we don't even know our own thoughts. Half the words we use have no meaning whatever and of the other half each man understands each word after the fashion of his own folly and conceit. Faith is a myth and beliefs shift like mists on the shore; thoughts vanish; words, once pronounced, die; and the memory of yesterday is as shadowy as the hope of tomorrow – only the string of my platitudes seems to have no end.'[8]

But these philosophical commonplaces, which were in the atmosphere of the times, can acquire a wholly other power if one takes them seriously, if one no longer treats them as philosophemes suitable for nourishing after-dinner conversations but instead as forms structuring a fictional space, if one shows *in actu* this indistinction between knowledge and ignorance, between action and passion, real and dream. That the real is not distinct from dream is something that can be read in two ways. After-dinner philosophers will conclude from it that life is but a dream, without this conclusion upsetting their digestion. But the novelist will draw a completely different consequence: if the real and dream are of the same substance, this means that there is but the real. It is on the basis of this identity that it is possible to understand the famous preface of *The Nigger of the Narcissus*, a novel devoted to an episode taken from the 'obscure lives of a few individuals out of all the disregarded multitude of the bewildered, the simple and the voiceless'.[9] The artist, it is written here, is not like the thinker or the man of science. These latter 'speak authoritatively to our common sense, to our intelligence, to our desire of peace or to our desire of unrest; not seldom to our prejudices, sometimes to our fears, often to our egoism – but always to our credulity'.[10] But the same cannot be said of the artist. The artist does not address our credulity, any more than our egoism, ambitions, fears or prejudices.

This inversion of roles, placing credulity on the side of science, may seem surprising. Its logic is nonetheless clear: the thinker and the man of science address themselves to minds that assess the chances there are for thought and desire to intervene in the external world, to minds that are concerned with order or with disorder, to minds that are fearful or super-stitious and need reassuring about the world's reality and about the aptitude of thought to attain its goals in it. They address themselves to positive minds, who need to believe because they need to plot the paths of the possible on the map of the real. The artist, for his part, is a sceptic, which does not mean he believes in nothing, or that he asks of his audience the favour of a 'suspension of disbelief'. Far more radically, he suspends the reasons themselves for belief, those that oblige us to distin-guish the probabilities of verisimilitude in the mixed fabric of thought and acts which makes up the consistency of experience.

Scepticism with regard to all operations of distinction goes
hand-in-hand with a solidarity with all lives whose reality itself
is condemned to indecision as to what is real and what dreamt,
to what is knowable and what unknowable. Scepticism thus
understood is 'the tonic of minds, the tonic of life, the agent of
truth – the way of art and salvation'.[11]

But this non-discriminating affinity does not simply define
the ethics of the artist. It determines the very texture of his work,
the appearance of new fiction. That dreams and acts are seized in
the same sensible fabric, and that the grasping of things 'as they
are' is itself a matter for words,[12] means that the veridical writer
deals with the real alone, with 'things as they are' and never
with things 'as they could be'. The critique of a colleague's work
furnished Conrad with the occasion to exclude from the domain
of fiction the category of the possible that founds representational poetics: 'everything in it is quite true and even obtrusively
possible – but not a single episode, event, thought, word; not a
single pang of joy or sorrow is inevitable. The end is an outrage
on the reader's intelligence not because the squire's daughter
marries the sergeant but because she marries that sergeant. It
would be just as logical to say she married a crossing sweeper
or the King of Monomatapa. Everything is possible – but the
note of truth is not in the possibility of things but in their inevitability. Inevitability is the only certitude; it is the very essence
of life – as it is of dreams. A picture of life is saved from failure

by the merciless vividness of details. Like a dream it must be startling, undeniable, absurd and appalling. Like a dream it may be ludicrous or tragic and like a dream pitiless and inevitable; a thing monstrous or sweet from which you cannot escape. Our captivity within the incomprehensible logic of accident is the only fact of the universe. From that reality ensues disappointment and inspiration, error and faith, egoism and sacrifice, love and hate. That truth fearlessly faced becomes an austere and trusted friend, a companion of victory or a giver of peace. While our struggles to escape from it – either through drink or philanthropy; through a theory or through disbelief – make the comedy and the drama of life. To produce a work of art a man must either know or feel that truth – even without knowing it.'[13]

There is only the real, that is to say a set of conditions – natural as much as social – whose ultimate connection escapes all mastery, as well as humans that turn this real into both the place of their daily bread and the theatre of their illusions – illusions that are themselves perfectly 'real' since they alone furnish humans with the reasons to live and act in this real. The stories that Conrad tells all pertain to a same fundamental schema: they are always born of an appearance, an illusion, a mistake. *Lord Jim* narrates the miserable fate of an individual dream of heroism, *Heart of Darkness* that of the great civilizing lie of the colonial enterprise. *Nostromo* is the portrait of a man who accepts to be paid solely in looks of admiration. *Under Western Eyes* develops the consequences of an optical illusion: in the reserved air of a student who dreams only of academic medals, revolutionaries persist in seeing the depth of thought of a soul complicit in their grand designs. But the story, we know, is only there to illuminate that which is all around, the sensible fabric within which the 'illusions' are produced and in which they have to produce their effects: a perfectly real milieu as a stage on which desires have to change themselves into acts, perfectly spectral at the level of the infinity of atomic connections that constitute the place and moment of the act, and those that weave the present of the subject whose act it is. In this milieu the story supplies the names of characters, places and situations. But it is from these properties that we must draw the necessity that assembles them into a fiction. This assembly can therefore no longer be a linkage in which actions transform situations and thus create the conditions for other situations and other actions. Conrad dismisses this logic by refusing to have the divisions of *Lord Jim* named chapters. A chapter of a novel makes the 'story' advance, but the milieu of the story does not advance. It is made up of beaches of light and mist each one of which is in the present. For it is only in the present of a scene that the clarity of the detail is assured – the detail alone is suitable to attesting that life is what there is and not the representation of a 'possible' story. The clarity of the detail is the texture of the inevitable: it is the decomposition of a situation and an action into the multiplicity of sensible events, which composes this situation's and action's perceptible reality; but it is also the limit placed on this decomposition, the punctuation of the encounter with the inconceivable that prevents this set of sensible events from constituting the rationality of a situation and sufficient reason of an action. Hence, the most famous scene of Conrad's most famous novel, the episode of abandoning the *Patna* in *Lord Jim*. The episode is made up of a multiplicity of sensible states and incidents that transform, first, the theatre of a possible action into a scene of passivity, before such passivity finishes with an act that itself exists only in the past. The story describes by turns: the great peace of the motionless sky and sea that sustain Jim's heroic dreams of action; the quarrel between the fleshy captain and the parched mechanic that confirms his feeling of being foreign to all that can happen in this world of mediocre individuals; the material collision of the ship's meeting with an unidentified obstacle; the sight, in the beam of a flashlight, of a hold submerged in water and a loose, rusty plaque that tells of the unavoidable shipwreck; the vain calculations of ways to save eight hundred passengers with seven lifeboats, leading to the passive resolution to wait calmly for the ineluctable end rather than trigger pointless panic; a look over the mass of bodies asleep on the bridge and heads that rise and fall in a jumble of crates, winches and fans; a black cloud engulfing the sky; a blow delivered by mistake for a pilgrim who simply asked for water for his son; a blow

unexpectedly received from the mechanic who mistook him for
a negro; the ridiculous and odious spectacle of the captain and
the mechanics getting entangled in their impatience to undo
a lifeboat to save themselves; the fall of one of the fugitives
suffering a heart attack; the grating noise of the davits starting
to turn and free the lifeboat; a jolt that seems to come from the
bridge and climb the length of Jim's back into his skull; the rustle
of the wind, a cry of pain, a jerky leg, the murmuring of voices,
the fugitives' calls to someone they are unaware is dead: a set of
noises and sights that befall Jim and that come to an end with
a bleat, a howl and a grunt, which create the call of the chasm
into which he throws himself, or rather is thrown, thus taking
the place of the accomplice that those voices were calling, and
also doing what he should have done in another circumstance,
in which the apprentice sailor's mistake was not to have jumped
at the right moment.

The 'impressionist' label readily tacked onto this type of story
ought not mislead us. The problem is not to put together the
whole of the picture by small strokes placed close together. The
course of sensible events reveals, on the contrary, the impossibility of the picture coming to an end. It could only do so at
the cost of attaining the ultimate truth of the real, that is, its
indistinction with dream. Ultimate reality is identical to the
song of sirens. To escape from it, one can only tie oneself to the
mast like Ulysses, circumscribe one's gaze and one's acts to the

circle of minor things to do be done, such as Marlow's caulking the leaky pipes of the boat heading up the Congo to resist the calls of bewitching dances from the shore, or such as Captain MacWhirr in *Typhoon,* who even prohibits the figurative use of language. But to one turned from this care of minor things by dreams of heroism, all that remains is to sink with Jim into the ocean of the inconceivable. Here is what distinguishes Jim's leap from the surrendering of Emma's hand. Flaubert built his atmospheric scene in concentric circles. From the distant choir of flocks, including orators and villagers, the wind brings the scattered tumult of sensible events into the centre where it is synthesized in the whirlwind of individual sensations leading one hand to surrender to another. The atmospheric dynamic of sensible accidents is thus inserted into the logic of the plot by accomplishing at once Emma's sentimental dreams and Rodolphe's prosaic calculations. This could be done since sensations were made thoughts and thoughts were made acts, in accordance with the modality of wish-fulfilment, or possibility. In Conrad, the totalization of sensible events is resolved only in the mode of the identity of the real and dream. And it is in accordance with this modality of the pure, irrational succession of real dream sequences that Jim jumps into the lifeboat, in an act that belies at once his heroic dreams, the mundane calculations of his companions and the positive rationality of facts awaited by the judges. Jim's jump belongs only to the order of the real, not to that of the possible. The great nebula of sensible states unfold only to mark the cut of the inconceivable that separates it definitively from the *possible* linkages of narrative action.

The Flaubertian compromise that subjugated the true description of sensible states to the artifice of causal fiction is thus no longer tenable. The description of sensible moments can no longer sprinkle the plot's path with its golden dust. It imposes a temporal construction that bursts asunder the normal temporality of progression of stories. Justifying his refusal to transform the breaks in the story into chapters, Conrad told his editor that all there is, is one episode. A single present is all there is. This present itself is of course woven from the encounter between the occasional hazards of circumstances, obsessive past fears and future anticipations inhabiting heads, in which the chimera pushing one to act is not separate from the positive reasons for action; and this past-present does not cease to haunt all the remainder of the story. But precisely these articulations of past, present and future, which ordered the time of fiction as a progression, have themselves gone over into a regime of coexistence. They are now internal to each present. This is also why this present itself is given through several narrative presents, each averred by the precision of the 'detail', such as in the court where this cloud of sensible events is judged in terms of positive facts and responsibility by a judge with his head inclined slightly on the shoulder, a first assessor with a thin horseshoe beard and a second drumming with his fingertips on a blotting-pad, while some flowers wither in a vase by the side of an inkstand;[14] in the front gallery of a dining-room where Jim tells his story to Marlow, seated at small octagon tables lit by candles burning in glass globes, in one of these cosy wicker armchairs separated by clumps of stiff-leaved plants, amidst the forest of red-shafted columns that sift out the sheen of the dark and glittering night, in which the riding lights of ships wink from afar.[15] The role of stories, and of stories about stories, in Conrad's great novels has nothing to do with any perspectivist relativism. It is a matter, on the contrary, of assuring the absolute truth of a present by renewing the mode of its presence. This is why Conrad reintroduces the function of the narrator that his master, Flaubert, made disappear during the first chapter of his first novel. And he does not hesitate to multiply the more or less plausible 'encounters' of the fictional narrator with the actors or witnesses of events. The plausible, precisely, is not his concern. The narrator's task is to ward off the distance that objective narration always institutes with this truth, and which the 'detail' alone guarantees. *Lord Jim* thus multiplies the presents that diffuse the book's sole 'event'. *Nostromo* builds a multiplicity of circles that work to cut and broaden the initial circle of a caricature event – a revolution by colonels in a South American republic – that is first perceived through the variations of noise and effects of light that the riot of the outside triggers inside a well-barricaded restaurant. Each of these circles serves to introduce the history of new characters involved in the situation. But each of these stories is attested only by the singularity of a vision and a noise. Hence the attesting of the decision that the young Charles Gould makes to recover the mine, whose silver is at the centre of the story, occurs through being made on a Tuscan Road at the hour of evening when the shadows of the chestnut trees, poplars and farm buildings lengthen, at the sound of a bell whose thin sound appears to set into the air the throbbing pulse of the setting sun.[16] And the development of the mine's activities is even evoked through the gaze directed, upon the hour of the shift change, at Indian boys leaning idly against lines of cradle wagons standing empty, screeners and ore-breakers squatted on their heels smoking long cigars, motionless wooden shoots slanting over the edge of the tunnel plateau and the noise of torrents mixed with the rumbling of turbines and stamps pounding on the plateau below.[17] Insistence on the details decidedly proves to be something entirely different to a 'reality effect', a tautological assertion replacing lost verisimilitude. It is rather an active destruction of this verisimilitude, a revolution in the ontology of fiction, which eliminates the gap itself between the real and the dream and substitutes the temporality of coexistences for the order of possible chains. But the 'merciless liveliness of the detail' is not simply the interminable journey through all the co-presences making up a situation. It is also the mark of what subtracts this situation from all mastery to make it the theatre of an 'adventure', that is to say, a random and inevitable encounter between a desiring and chimerical being and a reality whose synthesis escapes all calculation of causes and effects. It is the mark of the inevitable, which at any moment can bring the thinkable to tip over into the unthinkable, calculable danger into inconceivable horror and the chimeras of honour, justice or progress into the simple assumption of horror. The inevitability of the detail is the mark of these limit situations, emblematized by Jim's leap into the boat of infamy or Marlow's climb up to the place where the missionary of Western Enlightenment is in his death throes, and has become the most ferocious of ivory pillagers and the object of idolatory worship. Such situations are at the limit of the recountable, but they are also what is alone worthy of recounting and, at the same time, what can only be recounted, that is to say, transmitted by a voice that makes its own speech one with the experience of those men who had reached the limit of their chimera.

But can this revolution in the ontology of fiction remove the ultimate obligation to give the story a beginning, a middle and an end? Conrad's critics, who generally complain that he supplied a 'character study' instead of the action expected, also readily lament that he transformed this or that situation, which at most contained adequate material for a novella, into a whole novel.

Conrad himself presents the terms of the problem better. What merits being told can no longer be the undertaking of people seeking power, wealth or glory. It is singular and unpredictable moments in which the brilliance of a chimera encountering the unmasterable element of a situation comes to tear a hole in the routine of existence. It is 'the intensity of life, that light of glamour created in the shock of trifles, as amazing as the glow of sparks struck from a cold stone'.[18] Conrad places the evocation of this splendour in the mouth of Marlow, the narrator, who only mentions it himself in order to mark the impossibility of transmitting it to positive men, for whom listening to a story or reading a novel will only ever be a recreational activity for after dinner. The new story, the story that has revoked the reasons of verisimilitude, will always be at the limits of the transmissible and the intransmissible – and this is also one of the functions of this narrator, reintroduced by Conrad into fiction. Addressing his fictional audience, this mediator is tasked with underlining the limit between what can and what cannot be transmitted. But the distance that his character invokes quite clearly affects the novelist's task: how is one to order these presents of light and darkness, each of which is like a serpent curling in on itself, in the form of a story advancing toward an end? These encounters of accidents of life with the chimera which make living possible are without final word: 'there is never the time to say our last word – the last word of our love, of our desire, faith … truths'.[19]

To say the ultimate truth would be to do what the novelist has prohibited himself from doing: taking the role of the thinker who directs himself at the reader's 'credulity', when all he has to do is direct himself at his unconditioned sympathy for all humans who feel the joys and sufferings of their chimera. Neither Jim, Almayer nor Nostromo will proffer a last word. Kurtz, as we know, does state one – a word that says it all: 'horror'. But this saying-all cannot end the novel without betraying its principle, without addressing the 'credulity' that renders fiction pointless and that fiction renders futile.

There is no good ending. And yet the novel must have one. Is its only choice thus one between artifice and lie? The artifice is the *deus ex machina* that arrives from outside to put an end to a chimerical story that has no reason to stop. It is Brown the adventurer, who seems to disembark at Patusan only in order to provoke the spiral of murders that will claim Jim as a victim; it's the story of love and amorous jealousy between two sisters that arises unexpectedly at the end of *Nostromo* merely to provoke the case of mistaken identity as part of which a noble father fires a gunshot that claims the hero who was not the real target. But there is something even worse than the awkwardly grafted artifice designed to bring the interminable fiction to a close. There is the lie that denies its very principle. Such is, at the end of *Heart of Darkness,* Marlow's lie. His entire climb up to the Congo was like an inversion of the official fiction: that of the Western man's civilizing mission to abolish barbarous customs. By way of civilizing mission, Marlow saw a procession of chained-up Blacks, with iron collars round their necks, carrying materials up a sloping path for a needless railway; he smelt the odour of stupid rapaciousness and the dreams of ivory floating among idle Whites wandering with their long batons around these lost stations, which were supposed to be centres of human improvement; he perceived, at the bend in the river, the call formed, as though from the depths of the ages, by 'a burst of yells, a whirl of black limbs, a mass of hands clapping, of feet stamping, of bodies swaying, of eyes rolling, under the droop of heavy and motionless foliage'.[20] At the end of the track, he found skulls and crossbones adorning the fences of the missionary of progress who'd become the object of an idolatory cult and who exploited this cult to organize raids and appropriate all the country's ivory for himself. Marlow read on his report, vibrating with humanitarian eloquence, these simple words scribbled in the margins 'exterminate all the brutes' and he noted its last word: 'horror'. In returning Marlow merely had to carry out one last mission: go and see the fiancée who had held the sublime image of the civilizing hero in her heart and fulfil her last request: repeat to her the last words of this great soul, this talisman who helps her live. Marlow hears the very echo of the noises of his distant voyage in the low voice of the young woman: 'the ripple of the river, the soughing of the trees swayed by the wind, the murmurs of the crowds, the faint ring of incomprehensible words cried from afar, the whisper of a voice speaking from beyond the threshold of an eternal darkness.'[21] Yet the words consonant with that rumour of 'savagery', Kurtz's last words, are not the ones he will pronounce, but instead those the fiancée awaits: 'The last word he pronounced was – your name.' This word of the lying end of itself revokes the voyage that went to the true heart of the lie. The matter is not resolved by considering it as a concern not to drive to despair a soul in need of illusion. What is involved is the very possibility that the story tells the truth about the lie. The great scene of the sea and sky, of illusion and chasm on which Conrad shone the halo of obscure light is so far from the subdued light and the habits of thought specific to the places in which the stories are recounted that the very distance obliges one to lie in order to end the story and again to subtract the truth of sensible moments from the false tyranny of stories.

3

The death of Prue Ramsay

We must perhaps draw the paradoxical lesson of the matter: to make the luminous halo shine and to free its multiple splendour from the tyrannical authority of the plot, it is better to return the barometer portending great tumults of sky and soul to domestic space, in which all it indicates is the light that will colour the day or the outings that will be possible tomorrow. This is what Virginia Woolf does by reducing the plot to a minimum, to the point that the succession of things as they happen, one after the other, is almost confounded with the simple proceedings of a day or of a life: family stories that last the length of a day, with its changing lights and its varied tasks, or the length of a life, with the activities and the dreams specific to each age, from children's games to death including the university years, occupations of adulthood, marriage and maternity. The light of the lighthouse in sight marks the ultimate end of the voyage for James Ramsey; and the six characters of *The Waves* leave to the inconsistent hero of their dreams the risk of eastern adventure. But the familial restriction of the plot only radicalizes the tension. For the tyranny of the plot is itself a family affair. Tyrannical authority is first, of course, that of the father. The plot in *To the Lighthouse* is led by Mr Ramsay, who in the first part rules out the possibility of making the crossing, before going on in the third, to impose its necessity. But aside from the frank tyranny of the father, deciding what the day to come commands or prohibits, there is the soft, binding tyranny of the mother. The latter tyranny corrects the former, but in order to complement it. It arranges the great layer of coexistences that is opposed to the authority of links. But this is done in order to otherwise adapt it to the familial order, by reducing the anarchic shower of atoms to the small things and miracles of everyday life. How, then, is it possible to depict the luminous halo surrounding the fine plot of a deferred crossing by escaping from both sorts of tyranny? This is the question that the fictional artist Lily Briscoe asks herself, she who must escape not only from the matchmaking frenzy of the house's mistress but also from her 'binding attraction' in order to be able to grasp and set on her canvas 'that very jar on the nerves, the thing itself before it has been made anything'.[1] And this question is first and foremost, of course, one that arises for the novelist who wants to translate into words 'this thing itself', delivered of all the properties that practical usage or narrative utility confers on sense objects.

Well, *To the Lighthouse* advances a radical answer to this challenge in its second part, titled 'Time Passes'. This passing time, in effect, is not simply the interval of the war years during which the holiday house is left in a neglected state. It is an interval in which time acts by itself on things, produces events by itself, without being measured by the moments and scansions of any human activity or project. The succession of days and nights and that of seasons with their atmospheric variations, here determine events entirely delivered from the tyranny of human ends – absolutely impersonal sensible events. The essential characters of this section are the small detached airs of the central mass of wind, which passes via the rusty hinges and the panelling warped by humidity, sneaking in through the corner of the house before invading the empty rooms, playing with a tapestry, shaking the wall hangings, eating the wood and causing the casseroles to go rusty. The only significant events in the house are a plank falling on the landing, a shawl that comes free and dangles, shovelfuls of plaster falling off and a thistle slipping in between the paving stones. These sensible events that time alone produces in the house are explicitly opposed to those that stamp the course of human life and ordinarily compose the weft of fictions: stories of love, marriage or death, such as the sudden passing of Mrs Ramsay, or the joyous engagement and then distressing death of her daughter, Prue. In this chapter, these family events are granted the right, here and there, to two or three lines, and placed in square brackets so as better to underline their total heterogeneity to the sensible fabric of impersonal events. The identifiable events of personal life are properly placed in parentheses. This is also why, outside the hobbling old lady, who is periodically given the impossible task of resisting the invasion of time in the empty house, the only 'persons' who intervene in this section are themselves totally impersonal subjectivities, 'the wakeful' without identity, pure seers who wrench themselves from sleep to go and seek in the mirroring pools of water on the beach the remedy to the doubts of personal life, the light of this halo of which the mind only ever contains dispersed fragments. And this is exactly what the reflections in the pools of water seem to offer on some summer evenings: visions of 'flesh turned to atoms which drove before the wind, of stars flashing in their hearts, of cliff, sea, cloud, and sky brought purposely together to assemble outwardly the scattered parts of the vision within'.[2] These mirrors, in which the mind has become entirely impersonal, make very different calls than the baleful sirens that accompany Conradian travellers on their journeys. These are calls 'to range hither and thither in search of some absolute good, some crystal of intensity, remote from the known pleasures and familiar virtues, something alien to the processes of domestic life, single, hard, bright, like a diamond in the sand, which would render the possessor secure'.[3] But in vain does the text oppose the security of this impersonal diamond to the incident of domestic life symbolized by the death in square brackets of the unfortunate Prue Ramsay. The parentheses do nothing here. This dream of the absolute contemplated in the impersonal mirror of puddles of seawater is itself merely a 'reflection in a mirror'.[4] The autonomous time of the great impersonal life remains a parenthesis between two family scenes, between the evening of the outing's refusal and the morning of its enforcement. Events of fiction must always be ones that happen to characters who, at the same time, live the normal lives of individuals, who are mothers or daughters, husbands and wives, sons or fathers, meticulous housekeepers, amorous young people or solitary artists. The sensible milieu of fiction does not unfold its purity except as the milieu of a plot, a transition between its beginning and its end. The impersonal episode of *To the Lighthouse* will have above all served to sweep aside one of the two tyrannies, the most insidious one, the maternal tyranny that reduces the halo's fragments to familial virtues and the known pleasures of domestic life. Delivered from this temptation, the book's last part stages a new version of the tension between the democracy of the great impersonal life and the paternal tyranny of the plot. On the one hand, the artist, Lily Briscoe, is there, striving to capture the nervous vibration, the waves of the impersonal life traversing the artist's hand, on the canvas; on the other, there is, parting the real waves of the sea, the small boat taking the authoritarian father and the rebellious children to the lighthouse. Well, this voyage is itself a journey of reconciliation that will merit the rebellious son the supreme reward – his receiving of congratulations from the father for his skill in steering the craft toward its target. The fictional reconciliation with the father is also a compromise of new fiction with the necessity of the plot, a way of reconciling its beginning, middle and end. Most likely the irreconcilable singularity of sensation is reaffirmed in its rights with Lily's gesture of tracing on her painting the line that was necessary to completing it, the line that faithfully transcribes the shock of the 'thing itself'. But the line and the painting will never have been seen by anyone. They will have existed only in narrative sentences. They will have existed only to give new fiction the last word, to prevent the paternal seduction of the plot – which transforms ignorance into knowledge, unhappiness into happiness and hostility into reconciliation – from absorbing it.

Fiction, said Woolf, has no proper subject matter. Anything whatsoever can serve. Before her, Flaubert said that fiction had no 'subject matter' at all, that everything consisted in the absolute point of view of the style. But this absolute is precisely what causes the problem, this form whose properties must be the properties of the very fabric of sensible experience in its truth. The problem remains the same: if the whole is in the *kath' hekaston,* this means the whole proper to modern fiction consists in its phrasing. Fiction, however, cannot be dissolved into sheer music: the novel cannot be reduced to a long prose poem. It must always contain some arrangements of actions. The most natural arrangement of actions, then, is one that places its problem in the story, by making the tension between antagonistic figures of the whole the action itself. All of Woolf's great novels consist in this tension between several ways of inscribing the shower of atoms, several ways of making the halo shine and of comprehending the conflict opposing it to the logic of arrangement of actions. *Jacob's Room* tends to defer to the pure succession of moments, oftentimes reduced to the outlook of an outside observer. The three parts in *To the Lighthouse* construct the halo's relation with each of the figures of tyranny. *The Waves* offers the dream of 'a wandering thread, lightly joining one thing to another'.[5] But it is no matter of indifference that this is Bernard's dream. Bernard is the specialist of links, and is just as capable of striking up a conversation in a train with commercial travellers, as he is of seeking out in his notebook the fitting phrase for the present moment or of setting every face glimpsed behind a window to a story. His exceptional acumen does have its flipside: he can never finish his sentences, which remain suspended like a 'bit of string' and, regarding his stories, his friend Neville says that they can express everything, 'except of what we most feel', except the truth of what we feel.[6]

↬ The novel will therefore not be made of any single thread, not even a wandering one. It will be splintered between six subjectivities: from the inexhaustible inventor of stories, impervious to the halo, to the schizophrenic who feels it so strongly that she loses all possibility of stringing one sentence to another, including the sensible syntheses of the female lover, a friend of lights, or the mistress of the house, a friend of customs, the poet, a patron of forms, or of the melancholic, a lover of what is lost. But this mosaic will have to become monochromatic again in the last episode. When it comes to carrying the tale to its end, the creator of links and stories can alone take the floor.

But *Mrs Dalloway*'s seemingly smooth day probably shows best the dialectic whereby fiction is structured through its division. Indeed the straight line of time extending between the morning in which Clarissa Dalloway goes out to get some flowers and the evening of her party lends itself to two very different operations: a multiplication and a division. The first operation broadens the space of coexistences. The decision to go 'buy the flowers herself', announced in the first line, has, in fact, more consequences than it appears to here. If Flaubert liquidated the narrative subject in one chapter, then Virginia Woolf liquidated the subject of the narration – these manifestations of will that ordinarily determine the course of fiction via relations between characters – in a single phrase. Henceforth Clarissa will not be a centre in which the events of the sensible world come to condense. Such, it will be recalled, was Emma's position at the centre of circles that constituted the sensible universe of the fair. The dust trail of the carriage came to be concentrated, along with the whole universe of sensible coexistences, within Emma's subjectivity and with her given over to the logic of narrative and social identities. Things proceed totally differently with the noise of a motorcar and a plane's tracing of rings of smoke as they pepper Clarissa's walk. Far from bringing the spectacles of the city within her subjectivity, they retain their autonomy as sensible events, opening up an indeterminate space of subjectivation. They enable the narration to displace the line of the tale onto a multiplicity of anonymous lives that, for a time, receive a name and the possibility of a story. Such are, for instance, the passers-by that stop to decipher the letters of an advertisement that a plane is writing in the sky: Mrs Bletchley sees in the rings of smoke the word 'Kreemo', Mrs Coates reads 'Glaxo' and Mr Bowley thinks that it's 'toffee'. The arc continues with the young Maisie Johnson, who has newly arrived from Edinburgh to take up work in London; with the elderly Mrs Dempster's pondering both the hard life she's had and the beautiful feller that must be behind the plane's controls; with the unemployed seeker of truth's standing on the steps of Saint Paul's Cathedral, his bag bursting with pamphlets; and it eventually arrives at a quivering form, seen opposite a Tube station, sort of like a rusty pump or a wind-beaten tree, and whose voice, of no age or sex, is murmuring a chant with neither beginning nor end and deprived of any intelligible meaning. These anonymous lives are glimpsed. But the distance thus maintained precisely repudiates the tyranny of wanting to appropriate scarcely glimpsed faces by inventing stories for them. Such is how the far too clever Bernard operates, as does the female narrator of *An Unwritten Novel*, who reads a life of guilt and humiliation on the unhappy face of a female traveller before observing, upon the train's arrival, that the sad, forlorn creature is a mother with no story whose considerate son has come to collect her from the station. No such spoils are produced on Clarissa's walk. It opens onto these anonymous lives without absorbing them. In contradistinction, it is her own personal agenda that gets lost in the indeterminate circulation brought about by the spectacle of the street, the loops of a plane or the echoes of a song. Similarly with the evening walk that brings her former admirer, Peter Walsh, who chances upon the party venue, to discover along the way the half-hidden, half-apparent theatre of virtual stories: 'windows lit up, a piano, a gramophone sounding; a sense of pleasure-making hidden, but now and again emerging when, through the uncurtained window, the window left open, one saw parties sitting over tables, young people slowly circling, conversations between men and women, maids idly looking out (a strange comment theirs, when work was done), stockings drying on top ledges, a parrot, a few plants.'[7] The servant's idleness is the effect of a sensible revolution that this traveller discovers, having only recently returned from the Indies: the promoter of Summer Time, William Willett, had intended it to win an hour of work in the morning but to the walker it appears from the opposite angle: as an hour of daytime and leisure gained between work and sleep in the evening, an hour permitting anyone at all to enjoy the city's new amusements, but also the subjective experiences linked to the very disposition of time. This is the sensible democracy the walker senses, in 'suspecting from the words of a girl, from a housemaid's laughter – intangible things you couldn't lay your hands on – that shift in the whole pyramidal accumulation which in his youth had seemed immovable'.[8] The windows through which the walker perceives the infinite democracy of life constitute a response to the palace or carriage windows through which the elites of yesteryear kept commoners at bay so as to preserve for their refined feelings a vast space of interactions. Instead, the straight line of characters in attendance at a social engagement finds itself enlarged through the great democracy of perceptions and virtual stories, which line the walk and disseminate its sensible moments.

But this movement – which deflects a day in the life of this socialite toward the multiplicity of possible stories behind every window – is not enough to organize the relation between the luminous halo's truth and the plot's lie. It tends only to reduce it, to dissolve the plot's linking in the day of the city. But this dissolution is not enough to make shine the crystal of intensity intensity, promised to the wakeful by the reflections on the beach. For this, another operation is necessary: no longer a multiplication but, on the contrary, a division that contrasts sharply with the happy course of known pleasures and familial virtues, at the risk of setting off again the old mechanics that transform happiness into a misfortune. This second operation is allotted to a character, Septimus Warren Smith, a character that Clarissa never meets, except via one of her guest's talk at the party, and who is nevertheless her double, the unfortunate double whose inverse destiny provides inner closure to an all too open fiction. Septimus is the one who tears the happy fabric, formed by the rings of smoke, to answer the call that the wakeful read in the reflections of pools of water. He is the one who 'breaks the cord' of 'domestic life' by listening to the message addressed by sensible events: by the quivering leaves in the rush of air, the swallows swooping, swerving, flinging themselves in and out, or round and round with perfect order, the sun dazzling with soft gold now this leaf, now another, or the chime of a horn on the grass stalks. Mixed together, all these harmonies revealed to him, in their language of signs, the new religion: beauty is everywhere, and love, too: not the love of love stories and domestic virtues, but the universal love identical with universal life. Septimus draws the difference. To small miracles, felt while passing by in the street or glimpsing something behind a window, he opposes the great miracle of life of the universal One, which submerges the life of the

Ego. This great miracle has a name, unfortunately all too well known to Woolf: it is called madness. But this madness does not concern an individual biography. Its meaning must be forged within the economy of the new fiction. Septimus is not simply one who drowns in the puddle of water presenting the impersonal face of the vision within. It is also he who subjugates the impersonal life of the soul to a new personal plot: he deprives the puddles and clouds, the leaves and birds, the smoke in the air and reflections of light of their impersonality; he transforms them into signs announcing the new religion of the Chosen. And therewith is the tyranny of plot reintroduced into fiction. The Chosen becomes prey to another kind of tyrant, doctors. The latter are in fact expert at mastering this harmonious regulation between the impersonal aspect of life and the personality of individuals referred to as mental health; and in all naturalness does Virginia Woolf also turn them into champions of the old poetics: the Dr Holmes who plays the role of Human Nature and Sir William Bradshaw, the bard of Measure, goddess of classical Beauty and sister of the tyrant called Conversion.

Septimus will not escape the tyrants except by throwing himself out the window. His violent death denounces the artifice of the death in square brackets of the tender Prue Ramsay. To separate the lyricism of the great impersonal life from family stories, it is not enough to square bracket it. Separation pertains to the violence of the impossible. The diamond sparkles only in the brutality of the conflict between madness and normality. With Septimus's madness and suicide, tragic tyranny makes its return to the new fiction. But this return also structures the fiction, by making sparkle, at the heart of Clarissa's peaceful day, the collision of a mad truth with the plots of normality that ordain social relations and traditional-style fictions. One and the same madness hollows out the gap that prevents the luminous halo from being confounded with the small miracles of the everyday, and submits the shower of atoms to the constraints of the plot in which happiness is turned into misfortune. This is because neither the shower of atoms nor the luminous halo has a form that is proper to it. The ontology of the new fiction is monist, but its practice can only be dialectical: it can only subsist as a tension between the great lyricism of impersonal Life and the arrangements of the plot, a tension that does not escape modulations of compromise except at the cost of a violent sacrifice. The mad Septimus is a new incarnation of a figure essential to modern fiction: the personage that is perforce sacrificed in order to regulate the relation between the truth of the shower of atoms and the misleading logic of plots. The solution whereby the personage shoulders the burden of the lie was Flaubert's invention: it is Emma who will convert the dance of atoms into a sentimental story. This betrayal was sanctioned with her death. But this 'betrayal' was also necessary in order to reconcile the dance of atoms with the form of a story. Proust reconciled truth and lie in the same fashion. Albertine had to be killed so that the narrator could get rid of the illusion whereby an object of art – a splash of colour on a beach – is transformed into an object of love to be possessed. Septimus, as for him, is victim to the illusion whereby the reflections of light on leaves are transformed into a personal message. He joins the list of bad scriptwriters who misinterpret sensible events and for whom sin and punishment regulate the relation between halo-logic and plot-logic.

This sin, of course, has its cause. But it is an exemplarily split. Septimus is not only a victim of History's violence, a young man whose mental health was shattered by the trauma of the Great War. He is also, the novelist tells us, 'one of those half-educated, self-educated men whose education is all learnt from books borrowed from public libraries, read in the evening after the day's work, on the advice of well-known authors consulted by letter'.[9] Prior to the trauma that disturbs the soldier's mind, there is the gap inscribed in the vain distinction of that first name given to a child who bears the most common of surnames. There is the vanity of the autodidact who has created a culture by himself and fled his obscure provincial hole to seek out poetic glory in the big city where a certain Miss Pole, who taught classes on Shakespeare to the working classes, claims to see in him a brother of John Keats, the poet, son of a groom for horses, and sparked in him 'such a fire as burns only once in a lifetime'.[10] Even prior to being someone whom war has turned mad, Septimus is an incarnation of a well-known social figure: like Emma Bovary, but also like the Saint-Simonian dressmakers to whom their fathers had somewhat thoughtlessly given names such as Reine, Victoire or Desiree, or like their worker brothers dead from having wanted to be poets, he belongs to the redoubtable species of sons and daughters of the people who, instead of the life to which their birth had destined them, preferred that other life, the one promised in a few words written in books not intended for them. It is this new aptitude of the anonymous to live any life at all that permitted modern fiction to break with the hierarchical logic of action and to seek out its subject matter in any and every insignificant event. But this aptitude is something that modern fiction has also strived to put back in its place in order to separate the luminous halo of modern life from the personal aspirations of semi-educated common children. Emma Bovary had to be sacrificed in order to separate out the impersonality of art and the great equality of writing from petit-bourgeois aspirations to romance, to noble sentiments and to artistic surroundings. Septimus, too, is killed in turn, in order to create the chasm preventing the halo of light from losing itself in the agenda of a socialite. Novelists were to absorb the power of the anonymous into the impersonal breath of the sentence before then delivering this power over to the

tyranny of the plot. The poetic justice of modern fiction rests on
this primary injustice.

* * *

Some years later, a young reporter was probably pondering
this one summer evening while sitting under the canopy of a
house belonging to poor sharecroppers in Alabama. *Fortune*
magazine had sent him to see how people there were enduring
the Great Depression. On that night, however, James Agee had
something else in mind: the joy that can suddenly engulf you
'at any crossroads of time, of space and consciousness', thanks
to any among 'the number of unforeseeable hazards' that can
offer a ray of sun, plumes of smoke, the voice of a train in the
night, the burnt smell of fabric, the taste of turnip leaves and
thousands of sensible events of the same type.[11] In this halo
of light he could feel the intensity of life and beauty present
in any insignificant detail of the house decor of poor tenant
farmers: the light variations that, by turns, gave the boarding
the dazzling aspect of a silvery surface with 'shadows strong
as knives and India ink', and 'all slantings and sharpenings of
shadow', the aspect of bone or the colours of agate;[12] or else the
extraordinary texture of those overalls whose use and age, the
sun, sweat and laundering have made 'realms of fine softness
and marvel of draping and velvet plays of light', 'a region and
scale of blues, subtle, delicious' and of a deftness comparable

only 'to the smoky light some days are filmed with and some of the blues of Cézanne'.[13] But this capacity to see 'a great tragic poem' on a bedroom's pine boards or 'the feather mantle of a Toltec prince' on a pair of overalls mended a thousand times over, belongs to the writer and only to the writer. The flipside is the sharecroppers' own inability to see the beauty present in each knot of pine or each mending of overalls, through a lack of reason 'to see anything at all … in any way other than use and need'.[14] The ability to see all things in the light of the halo is a privilege founded on their dispossession.

The dialectic at work here is more complex, however. This ability, which separates the writer from the tenant farmers, also enables the former to subtract the latter from another form of appropriation, the power of appropriation of the media that had sent him there to collect signs enabling these sharecroppers' lives to be rendered immediately legible and intelligible; the power integrate these lives to integrate them into the verisimilar tale of social necessity that it periodically offers its readers to digest. For journalism in the twentieth century is the great Aristotelian art. It constructs reality according to a schema of verisimilitude or necessity, or, more precisely, a schema that renders verisimilitude and necessity identical. The reporters, sent to meet the poor inhabitants of the deep country, thus had to combine the markers of individual reality averred by the tale, together with signifiers of statistical generality, which show this reality to conform to what is known, to conform to what it cannot not be. This identity of the verisimilar and the necessary constitutes the heart of what we call consensus. But this verisimilar and necessary agreement of reality and its sense is precisely what modern fiction smashed to pieces through its use of the 'detail'. And this is the school in keeping with which reporter James Agee undertook to sabotage the assignment. His painstakingly detailed inventory of the items kept in each drawer of each piece of furniture in the Gudger house, his effort to capture the light and odour of the oil lamp, the grain and smell of the pine slats and the breathing of sleeping bodies – all this ruins every process whereby traits are selected in order to make the lives of tenant farmers consumable for the media machine. By accentuating, on the contrary, the absolute singularity of their existence and by linking this with the infinite multiplicity of these 'atmospheric' events, shown by modern fiction showed to be present in every minute of the universe, he tears them from the place they are assigned in the consensual order and restores them to a level of shared humanity.

In this way the dialectic of modern fiction becomes more complex. It appropriates the unprecedented capacity of the anonymous in order to forge its own power, the impersonal power of writing. But in the same stroke it also forges a power of rupture with consensual logic, which keeps anonymous lives in their place; it forges a power of dissolution of consensual identities, situations and sequences, which only work to reproduce, in modern clothing, the old hierarchical distribution of forms of life. This dialectic is perhaps interminable.

PART TWO

THE REPUBLIC OF THE POETS

4

Spider's work

Among the working-class children whom the power of words had seized and who attempted works of writing and thought to which their birth and education had not destined them, at least one has entered the Pantheon of great poets: John Keats. The elements of his biography are well known: he was the son of a hostler who died when the young John was barely eight years old; for want of humanist assimilation in the colleges of well-born children, he studied in an establishment open to modern ideas, prior to being placed, upon the death of his mother, as an apprentice with an apothecary; the son of the head of the establishment introduced him into a circle of liberal artists and thinkers who supported the cause of working-class people fighting for their thwarted political rights. And this is the circle that enabled him to embark on a poetic career. It is evident, however, that this social journey is not enough to define the politics of a poetry. And there are two judgements about John Keats's politics that divide the field. One of them notes that if the sympathies of Keats the individual side clearly with the radical cause, we do not encounter in his poems either Wordsworthian claims about the dignity of the humblest beings and things, or Shelley's or Byron's calls to rebellion against the social order, but instead a dream of ageless beauty proclaiming its self-sufficiency. The other responds that the purity of the poem is better isolated when its context is ignored. Well, the famous ode *To Autumn* was written in September 1819. The previous month in Manchester had seen the savage repression of a demonstration for electoral reform that became known as the Peterloo Massacre. And a read of the September issue of the *Examiner*, Keats's friend's own newspaper, is enough to see, through the mediation of a poem by Spenser, a clear equation established in it between the abundance of harvests and the just distribution of the produce of labour, as symbolized in the symbol of the balance.[1] In reply it can nevertheless be stated that, even if such concerns weighed on Keats's own mind, the 'justice' of the poem is defined through another balance: a paradoxical set of scales in which the season of mists is equated with that of fruits, and the regenerative activity of autumn with the indolence of a divinity sitting insouciantly on a granary floor or drowsed by the fume of poppies on a 'half-reap'd furrow'.

The season of fruits does not, then, symbolize the poem's commitment to serving the creative labour of wealth and justice.

But, conversely, neither does the goddess's calm repose signify the consecration of a classic and serene ideal of beauty, unconcerned by political and social turbulences. What gives the poem not meaning but place is the very relation between mist and fecundity, sleep and creative activity. This identity of contraries defines the poem's relation to its subject and this subject's relation to all that it is permissible to associate with it – time's passing or nature's ageless fecundity, dreams of a golden age and figures of mythological landscapes or the reality of men's labour. It defines it because it defines the poem itself as a certain weaving of the material and the immaterial, of passivity and activity. What this weaving determines, then, is not the relation of the poet *with* politics, or the presence of politics *in* the poem. It is the politics itself *of* poetry, the way it configures the space in which it inscribes its productions. It does this by instituting a triple community. This is, first, the community among the elements from which poems are woven: the words and presences they stir up – fragrances of flowers in fields or palaces built in the clouds, familiar bird songs or pages from mythology textbooks; it is the figures, the stories that assemble them, the universes that they deploy or the rhythms accompanying their appearings and their disappearings. Second, it is the community among these poems and other poems: those that the poet has written and those he has not: that is, the ones that will remain visions of his mind – reveries of idleness or dreams of night, the ones that others have written and from which he takes nourishment as others do of his; the ones, lastly, that the new sensibility of the age of revolutions already sees present in all manifestations of life. One of Keats's teachers, William Hazlitt, recalled this by way of introduction to his public courses on the English Poets: poetry exists before words; it exists as the capacity of human beings to feel the poetry already manifest in a wave's motion or a flower's unfurling. It is already present in children's games, in the countryman's gaze upon the rainbow or in the city-apprentice's view of the municipal parades.[2] And with this the third form of community is instituted: one that the poem's specific mode of sensible communication projects as a possible relation between humans. The politics of the poem can thus be defined as the configuration of a specific sensorium that holds these three communities together.

In fact, few poets have felt as keenly as Keats that poetic activity consists in this weaving. But probably none have ever linked this community vocation as radically to solitary reverie and brought this act as close to pure inactivity. Attesting to this is the extraordinary letter to John Reynolds dated 19 February 1818, in which poetry – far from the reverie of art for art's sake – is defined as a way of living, thinking, acting, communicating and, ultimately, of forming a community. We are familiar with its abrupt opening: 'I have an idea that a Man might pass a very pleasant life in this manner – let him on any certain day read a certain Page of full Poesy or distilled Prose and let him wander with it, and muse upon it, and reflect from it, and bring home to it, and prophesy upon it, and dream upon it – untill it becomes stale – but when will it do so? Never.'[3] Poetry is not first a way of writing but a way of reading and transforming what one has read into a way of living, of turning it into the support of a multiplicity of activities: strolling about and dawdling, reflecting, making an exegesis, dreaming. It is true that the very word 'activity' invites discussion. Dream seems to be a state rather than an act; and vagabondage and playing games, though they set body and mind in movement, lack what classically characterizes action, which is the pursuit of a goal of which this movement is the means. From reading, which gives impetus, to the ethereal dream, in which the chain of metamorphoses comes to an end – or rather continues to infinity – the series of actions seems to be eaten into by its contrary, passivity. The phrase that follows confirms this with a gripping oxymoron: the 'journey of thought' is the work of a 'diligent indolence', as illustrated by the following series: a rest on a sofa, a nap upon clover, childish babble, a conversation, a voyage on the wings of music that, like Ariel, transports the spirit to all places, and that, like Puck, makes the trip around the world in forty minutes. But the oxymoron can be read in both directions. Poetic indolence is likened to the work of an insect whose industrious activity is also a model of artistic composition. By imitating the spider, which gains its support on the extremities of leaves or twigs, the poet is able, out of practically nothing at all, to weave his celestial tapestry. Indeed, it is not enough to say with Hazlitt that poetry is everywhere where humans pursue a dream, be it the miser's dream of money or the prince's dream of glory.[4] Poetry can belong to all as a common fabric, constantly rewoven from such or such a fragment (*parcelle*). To achieve this the diligence of dreamy spiders is thus required; spiders whose work is rid of its utilitarian, that is to say, predatory, function.

This confusing of work and rest, of purposive activity and aimless reverie bears witness to the great upheaval of conditions and thoughts produced by the revolutionary age. This age in actual fact contains two lessons, diametrically opposed to each other: one is that the first plebeian come may, through his intelligence and will, become the ruler of Europe; the other is that, if he gives up the pretension to command others through his will, the first plebeian come may enter into conversation with the gods and their poets. There is a subversive virtue in the fact of not acting or rather of rendering action inactive and inaction active. In order to think through this equivalence of contraries, the poet Keats forged another oxymoron, that of *negative capability*: not a negating capacity but a 'capacity not to': not to seek the reason, but also: not to conclude, not to decide, not to impose.[5] Like the autumn that leaves its sickle at rest, the poet must keep himself from having 'any palpable design on us'.[6]

To refuse the approach that seeks to take hold of others' minds, as the insect does its prey, is the principle of this new relation to things of poetry and art called aesthetics. Schiller formulated it brusquely: 'Nothing is more hostile to the concept of beauty than the will to give a determinate tendency to the spirit.'[7] Greek art's greatness, for him, is that of a free people, a people whose supreme activity is play, which is its own end. This is why, he adds, this people sculpted those gods whose faces express no will or bear any concern to accomplish an end. This refusal of all determinate tendencies has nothing to do with an apolitical love of pure beauty. It founds, on the contrary, a new 'art of life', an education of each and all. What beauty demands and nourishes in return is the formation of a sensible capacity untied from the means and ends of the will. And this suspensive capacity disrupts the traditional distribution of bodies in community: not only does it arrest the hand that takes, the act that orders and the brain that imposes the will of the powerful; it annuls the hierarchy of ends that, since time immemorial, had divided the world into two between those who could have no end other than the day-to-day reproduction of their existence and those who, being sheltered from this vital constraint, could conceive more ample ends, invent their means and risk undertaking them. These latter could, for the same reasons, just as easily do nothing or else dedicate themselves to activities that were their own end. Indeed the supreme good consisted precisely in this. Well, aesthetic capacity puts this privilege of the chosen at the disposal of all: Winckelmann's inactive Hercules, the reverie or idleness of Rousseau's solitary walker, Kant's 'finality without end', Schiller's play drive – all designate a hitherto unseen 'capacity not to do anything', which revokes this sensible difference between two humanities. Keats had hardly read the Germans and had little sympathy for Rousseau. However, his 'Endymion', a dreamer visited by the moon, fits squarely within the lineage of inactive gods celebrated by Winckelmann or Schiller. But 'negative capability' also radicalizes the aesthetic suspension by putting the identity of the personal and the impersonal at the very heart of the poetic act.

It is certainly understood, since Vico, that the infant Greek people speaks in Homer's verses, since Winckelmann, that Greek liberty is embodied in the undulations of the *Torso de Belvedere,* and, since Schiller, that the health of a playful people is expressed on the serene face of the *Juno Ludovisi.* But it is the figure of the rhapsodist declaiming before the people, or of the sculptor extracting from a block of marble the figure of the city's gods, in which the ideal relation between individual act and the collectivity is embodied. Keats, himself, kept a distance from these images of embodiment. During his self-education he had gained familiarity with the Greeks, via the mediation of Elizabethan-era translations and transpositions. His interest thus bore not on the relation of Homer or Phidias to the Greek city, but instead on the availability of works, on the possibility, for each individual, of integrating them into a chain of equivalences, freely woven between hours of reverie and pages of an old translation, verses written by the great poets or fabulous tales, trails of clouds or the song of a thrush, and evocations of distant times and countries. This is how the personal and the impersonal encounter one another. They do so in the reader's reverie, which submits any old extract of 'noble poetry' to the infinite series of transformations that will raise him to the conquest of the 'two-and-thirty palaces'; and again in the spider's web that this reader/poet can himself weave for all to benefit from by beginning from a small number of points of contact: some singular sensations, perhaps similar to the bubbling up of water through a reed, to the feather and twig boats that the child sails on it, or to the fanciful cloud forms reflected in it.[8] To spin the web is not to weave sensations into an embroidery likely to ensnare the reader; it is to make them into points of departure, able to engender the multiplied circles in which are awakened for some other reader or dreamer forgotten names, legends and wonders, ancient airs imprisoned in tombs or the spectres of melodious prophecies revelling (*délirant*) 'Round every spot where trod Apollo's foot'.[9] Rather than Schillerian free play *vis-à-vis* free appearance, poetic disinterestedness is the work of an imagination that continually takes from and gives to the common fabric.

But this relation between the personal and the impersonal is assured only if poetic weaving maintains the line of equivalence between the active and the inactive. The weaving of words, images and rhythms on the page escapes the author's vanity and the despotism of 'palpable designs' only if he keeps his community with the imagination that dissipates like the reverie of an autumn afternoon or a summer's night dream. This reverie does not succumb to the condemnatory blow that, in *The Fall of Hyperion,* contrasts dreamers with poets.[10] For those the goddess calls 'dreamers' are not the idle who pursue the two-and-thirty palaces. They are, on the contrary, those who want to affirm their dream, turn it into a 'palpable design' to impose on others. What characterizes poets is a twofold refusal: that of making the poem the mark of their identity; and that of giving to their dream the character of an affirmation. The poem is such only if it is 'by nobody'. But it is only 'by nobody' if its act is scarcely distinguishable from inaction, if the diligence of verse work shares the same sensible ideality as the indolence of reverie. This sensible multiplicity takes a multiplicity of names – visions, forms, figures, shadows or phantoms – which evoke different modes of materiality. If shadow is bereft of form's affirmed perceptual certitude, its power of evoking stories and vanished worlds is better able to nourish the work of the web. And the fertility of autumn, just like the 'joy forever' constructed by spider's work, are sisters of the passivity that listens without anything identifying anything to the song of the nightingale. *Ode on Indolence* even bids that poetry itself vanish among the clouds, together with those other phantoms of love and ambition, since it is unable to offer him a joy 'so sweet as drowsy noons / And evenings steeped in honeyed indolence'.[11] Just as the exercise of power in Plato, so, too, for poetry in Keats: the only ones fit to do it are those who know a higher good. Many others subsequent to Keats will proclaim the work's impersonality. But they do so only to oppose, like Flaubert, its solidity, as open to all, to the inner flow of feeling. Keats's singularity is to have affirmed that the 'inner citadel' itself is just as impersonal as it is personal: extended between the immemorality of legends, the great 'passive' fabric of already written poems, sleep's loss of consciousness and dream's unconscious life.

To him is due the thought of this tension as a specific form of equality: the equality of the web that extends to infinity without experiencing any summit or base, or other side or place. This equality here is clearly opposed to another: that which recognizes in each insignificant flower a subject worthy of poetry and in each peasant, pedlar or beggar the bearer of a divine spark. This latter equality provides the framework of *The Excursion*, the long poem by Wordsworth that the young Keats counted among the joys the era offered. In the poem's last song, the 'Sage' wants to show to the 'Solitary', who is filled with the nostalgia of

disappointed revolutionary promises and is distressed about the
persistent spectacle of popular misery, another promise, namely
that present in the manifestations of equality everywhere offered
in the visible universe:

> Throughout the World of sense
> Even as an object is sublime or fair
> That object's laid to the view
> Without reserve or veil […]
>   The smoke ascends
> To heaven as lightly from the cottage-hearth
> As from the haughtiest palace. He whose soul
> Ponders this true equality, may walk
> The fields of earth with gratitude and hope.[12]

Sun, which descends to enlighten the great and the humble;
smoke, which climbs the thatched cottage and the palace alike
– this equality is immediately verticalized. If the walking poet
moves, it is to find equality everywhere the same, offered to all
by the divinity, who has granted each form of being an 'active
principle'.[13] Equality is given from above, and the poem rounds out
in an educational programme for the people, which ascends like a
prayer toward the heavens toward 'the paternal ear of the state'.[14]

Concerning this equality, Hazlitt's lectures, even prior to
Wordsworth's official rallying behind the Tory camp, were
probably what led Keats to see its other side: the great equality of

all and of all beings that the Lake poets proclaimed allows only one superiority to subsist in the world: that of the poets who've proclaimed it.[15] The letters written to Reynolds in February 1818 were manifestly written under the shock of this revelation. They draw from it the radical conclusion. Equality must be thought as integrally horizontal. Stretched out on a sofa or on clover, the dreamer in his indolence or passivity participates in this inversion. This stands in contrast with the approach of the walker who carries around with himself the 'active principle', granting equality to passers-by as sovereigns grant charters to their people. The shadow of the Wordsworthian walker lurks over Keats's Scottish travels of summer 1818 and explains their constant irony: on the roads of the Highlands no vagabond or pedlar with sublime thoughts was crossed, but instead rain, mud, oat bread, the sourness of whisky and suffo-cating smoke in shepherds' shacks. And, instead of encounters with philosopher pedlars, it was rather the poets out hiking with their backpacks who were (mis)taken for spectacle vendors, razor sellers and travelling linen drapers.[16] Equality's journey is not made on country roads. It is undertaken lying down in a state of indistinction, between activity and passivity, percep-tions and evocations, wakefulness and sleep, personality and impersonality, life and death. This journey does not discover any presence of creative divinity in the modest petals of the celandine or in the wisdom of a pedlar that the years and burden have worn out. It participates in divine equality when it allows visions to follow their shadowy journey freely between reverie, urn and poem, and allows the nightingale's song in the dark night of May to join together with the song Ruth once heard in the fields of Boaz or with the song that has so often 'charmed magic casements in faery lands forlorn'.[17] Christian equality, celebrated by Wordsworth, turns each individual into an image of the divinity. Keats's 'paganism' refuses these embodiments and, freeing sensations from any personal identification, renders them in their state as parading shadows, as voices that go from hedge to hedge like grasshoppers or run from age to age and, like the nightingale, cross the frontiers of the real and legend. This is also why, against the grain of what had appeared the great advance of the Romantic age, Keats restores the characters and mythological scenes that Chateaubriand had charged with diminishing nature and from which the poetry of Wordsworth and Coleridge had freed the fields and forests. Remythologizing nature, in return, frees it from the dependence of each sensation as regards its subject and of each creature as regards its creator, which transforms poetry into an egotistical parade and sermon. To this 'sentimental' destiny of modern poetry, Schiller had opposed the 'naïve' poetry of the Ancients. Naïve poetry was not that which made truth issue from the mouths of peasants, pedlars or beggars; instead, it bore on nature as not separated from culture, whose copses prepare to welcome the conversation of philosophers and laurels, to gird the heads of athletes and poets. This is the cost at which the poem on the page belongs to all – the sensation it arouses in the daydreamer stretched out on the sofa or patch of clover resuscitates a past, prophetizes a future, or serves as the departure point for a web of sensations, of appearing and disappearing shadows, and of heard and unheard melodies, which are at once the private garden of the idle and the diligent spider's gift, offered to whomever wants it. One can discover everywhere, says the Christian poet, the active principle that connects each thing to its heavenly creator. One can discover everywhere, retorts the pagan poet, the fragment of inactive and impersonal life that leads to the two-and-thirty palaces of the imagination and is connected, step by step, but also interminably, to the life of the whole.

At the time the young English poet was elaborating his poetic programme, a French professor, Joseph Jacotot, exiled in Belgium upon the return of the Bourbons, was elaborating the mad thoughts that, ten years later, would provoke panic in the savant world: everything is in everything and all intelligences are equal. In every phrase written on paper one can find the point of departure that will enable the ignorant to enter the realm of writing and commence an endless apprenticeship. This phrase could be the first sentence of Fénelon's *Telemachus*: 'Calypso remained inconsolable for the departure of Ulysses.' It could be a fragment of a prayer or of a calendar. The essential thing is to set off, to act as a researcher does in being attentive to all the signs a hand has traced or all the surrounding words, and also as an artist does by assiduously arranging signs suitable to speaking to another intelligence: the method is 'panecastic', he says, i.e. a way of recognizing in *each* manifestation of intelligence the *whole* of its powers; a way, also, of instituting an equality that has nothing to do with what the laws or state may decree. This equality indeed exists only if it is always in act, stretched between one word and the next, one voice and another, an intelligent being and another intelligent being.[18] By the time the voice of the exile from Louvain began to be heard, the young poet's body will have been long buried in the protestant cemetery in Rome, and their writings will never have crossed each other. However, something is commonly affirmed in them, something that belongs not to this or that individual but to the reflection of the times, to the assessment of the great revolutionary upheaval to which the triumphant restoration obliges: an idea of equality that is first one of fragments, sensations or signs all equally animated by the power of the whole; a practice of the web traced step by step to extend infinitely the power of a singular assemblage of these sensations or these signs; a faith in the capacity present in each person to weave such a web for himself, by clinging to the points of all the leaves, put at his disposal by an infinity of others; a vision of the community that can be sketched thus: a community of people in full possession of a sensible equality

experienced in the singularity of encounters and communications and not in the universality of laws. All intelligences are
equal, said Jacotot. Keats's assertion in his letter to Reynolds
echoes this statement: almost anyone can be the spider who
weaves his own citadel in the sky, or the false question raised
at the start of *The Fall of Hyperion:* 'Who alive can say, / "Thou
art no Poet; mayst not tell thy dreams"?'[19] Humans are political
animals because they are poetic animals and by striving to
verify shared poetic capacity, each person for him- or herself,
they are able to establish a community of equals. The letter to
Reynolds thus inverts the classic argument of good sense: how
will individuals, left free to weave their web in any direction they
please, be able to avoid pulling in all directions? How can 'any
common taste and fellowship' exist between them? To this good
sense the poet answers that it is precisely at the crossroads of this
multitude of individual journeys, of singular weavings of the
common wealth, that a new common sense may be elaborated.
This link between a faculty of feeling and a faculty of communicating, specific to humanity as such, had preoccupied minds for
some decades already. A great reader of Rousseau, Kant worked
on redefining the 'humanities' proper to the enjoyment of the
Beaux-Arts: 'Humanity means on the one hand the universal
feeling of participation (*Teilnehmungsgefuhl*) and on the other
hand the capacity for being able to communicate one's inmost
self universally'[20]; and he saw in this universal faculty of sharing

an intimate principle of rapprochement between the sensible manners of the cultivated classes and those of the uncultured classes, thus preparing for a new sociability. From this Schiller drew the idea of an aesthetic education that would answer the revolutionary age's plea for a new humanity. And for Keats the individual journeys of poetic animals leads properly toward an aesthetic democracy: 'Minds would leave each other in contrary directions, traverse each other in Numberless points and all last greet each other at Journey's end – An old Man and a child would talk together and the old Man be led on his Path, and the child left thinking – Man should not dispute or assert but whisper the results to his neighbour, and thus by every germ of Spirit sucking the sap from mould ethereal every human being might become great, and Humanity instead of being a wide heath of Furse and Briars with here and there a remote Oak or Pine, would become a grand democracy of Forest Trees.'[21] Once again the encounter of the old man and the child must be seen with reference to Wordsworth. The old man here neither testifies nor moralizes. He is only strengthened in his path. The child is neither saved nor educated, but is left to his thought, to the pensiveness that consists in the refusal to conclude and that literature, during the times of Hugo and Flaubert, will affirm as its supreme power. Not to conclude, not to affirm, but 'to murmur', akin to the wind in the leaves, leaves between which the spider's web is woven; such, the poet affirms, is the mode of communication specific to the formation of an effective, sensible democracy.

The vegetal metaphor is obviously overdetermined. Trees and leaves are indeed at the core of inegalitarian rhetoric. First, leaves; since Leibniz we've know that, despite appearances, no two of them are alike. And this dissimilarity, inscribed in the very life of vegetal nature, serves as a sufficient argument to all those who denounce the gruesome utopia aiming to render equal those infinitely more complex beings that are humans. But the argument is specious. For who exactly is the one concerned with comparing leaves? The true question is to know what sets them in community. On this point even the writer that hates equality and fraternity can discover himself a democrat in his practice. To wit, Flaubert's letter to Louise Colet, in which he proclaims himself an 'enraged aristocrat', rounding out his demonstration as follows: 'I am certain, incidentally, that men are no more brothers to each other than the leaves of woods are the same. They [the leaves] are tormented together, that's all.'[22] But it is this 'that's all' which forms all: that 'common torment' which is communicated from leaf to leaf and that will be communicated to the reader of Flaubert, because the novelist, who does not know its origin, has communicated it to his provincial petit bourgeois character. In the same way, the equality of leaves in Keats is the equality of breath communicated from some to others and of webs woven between all their tips.

HUMANS UNDERSTAND Themselves relationally - That is their Common Ground.

As for trees, we know that, since Burke, great oaks were
made the very symbol of the harmonious world that revolutionary madness had destroyed: a community conceived as a
great park in which higher powers extend their protective shade
over the little people. In its wake an entire century will not
stop lamenting that, with its sovereign oaks uprooted, society
has become a democratic copse of puny trees that strangle
each other and stifle all greatness – whether it be the glory of
peoples or of art, both of which require the broad perspectives
offered by landscapes organized around grand tutelary trees for
development. Well, here again, Keats brutally inverts common
opinion: under the isolated oaks of aristocratic majesty all that
exist are brambles and gorses. Instead of desolate lands, a still-
unknown forest of democratic trees can rise through the work of
each germ of mind sucking the sap of a celestial humus. This also
means that Keats displaces the great Romantic idea of poetry as
the flowering of the life of a people. It is pointless to want to give
flesh to the procession of figures of the Greek urn, to imagine
poetry as a religious or civic celebration, the public manifestation
of an organic life of the people. The ceremony's participants have
gone; the city is empty. What remain are the procession of ideal
figures around the urn and the idleness nourished with their
presence/absence and that with it nourishes the poetic rhythm
that today is their only actuality. Poetry is not the flourishing
of any people; it is the incessant exchange between the inaction

of the dreamer, the labour of the insect and the offering of the
flower by which the web of a people to come is perhaps woven,
a people of poets such as the thinker of emancipation would
dream it to be: a hitherto unseen community of individuals
seeking means to join up together through the forest of signs
and forms, a community constituted at the risk of multiple
journeys and encounters under the sign of equality.

5

The infinite taste of the Republic

During summer 1851, the twentieth instalment of the edition of Pierre Dupont's *Chants et Chansons* came out. It contains a prefatory note dedicated to the author and signed 'Charles Baudelaire'. The latter was not satisfied with a polite tribute to a fellow-poet and friend. He turned his note into a poetic and political manifesto against Romantic 'voluptuousism' and the 'puerile' and 'sterile' utopia of art for art's sake. Pierre Dupont's poetry, for him, was not merely the painful expression of the 'sickly multitude that breath workshop dust' and 'sleep in vermin'. By including the 'long look full of sadness' that this multitude casts on 'the sun and shade of the great parks', it expresses much more profoundly the 'genius of humanity' and the 'higher principles of universal life'. The secret of Pierre Dupont's poetry resides not in its technical skill. It resides 'in the love of virtue and humanity, and in that *je ne sais quoi* that radiates constantly from his poetry, which I would gladly call the infinite taste of the Republic.'[1]

The claim that these Second Republic-style humanitarian hyperboles are an interlude in the life of a poet, for whom the barricades of 1848 served primarily as an outlet for familial furies and who therefore did not waste any opportunity to mock the religion of progress and affections for the woes of the people, is probably founded. But even more so is the insistence that this revolutionary interlude is the only time that the poet got involved in politics and that, in the midst of this 'lifelong abjuring' to which he claims every 'system' condemns those who shut themselves within it,[2] he showed himself to be unswervingly faithful to certain friendships and constant in his predilections for specific theoreticians and artists who undeniably present features of Republican poetry, social criticism or humanitarian religion: David, Barbier, Dupont, Proudhon, Leroux and Chenavard. The point being that the dogmatic will to establish the criteria of the beautiful always lags behind when it comes to 'universal humanity' and to 'multiform and multi-coloured Beauty, which moves in the infinite spirals of life.'[3] The 'infinite taste of the Republic' is not a circumstantial political infatuation against which this poet-aesthete would later oppose the aristocracy of art for art's sake. It is a category of the aesthetic itself, of an aesthetic politics, and the new disciple of Joseph de Maistre has no problems appealing to it when, in the midst of total imperial reaction, he has to give a report on the art of painters. 'Universal life' and the 'genius of humanity' innervate the report the poet wrote for the 1859 Salon and the reflections he drew from it as to the essence of modern art. And these notions establish a singular line of egalitarian union between two characters that one would have thought destined never to meet: on the one hand, the painter of elegant life whose gaze delights in 'fine carriages, proud horses, the dazzling clean-liness of the grooms, the dexterity of the footmen, the sinuous gait of the women, beautiful children, happy to be alive and well dressed – in a word, who enjoys universal life';[4] on the other, that German peasant, who asked a painter to portray him on the threshold of his farm at the day's end, together with his large family, the signs of his prosperity and puffs of his pipe hued by the setting sun, without forgetting to render 'the air of satis-faction' he felt in contemplating his wealth's having 'increased by the labours of a day'. Contrary to the 'spoilt children' of painting, confined within the technical skill of the profession, this peasant here, Baudelaire comments, 'understood painting. The love of his profession had heightened his *imagination*.'[5] That the child of the peasant and of the wealthy man each have an equal air of satisfaction is the reflection of the common wealth, of the participation in 'universal life', which is missing in Theodore Rousseau's 'glistening marsh' or Boudin's 'liquid or aerial conjurings'. To denounce this lacuna, Baudelaire has no hesitation in appealing to the authority of a most unlikely judge in matters of art, Maximilien Robespierre, who, having 'carefully studied his humanities', knew that humans 'are never without pleasure in seeing others'.[6]

The 'infinite taste of the Republic' is therefore not an ephemeral expression from times of political fever. It is the enduring formula of an aesthetic republicanism. To draw out its features, we must mark a distance with today's dominant interpretation of Baudelaire, the Benjaminian one of the 'lyric poet in the era of high capitalism'. Through all its variations, this interpretation obeys the same fundamental objective. It aims to link the thematic and rhythm of Baudelairian poems directly to an anthropological given constitutive of modernity: that of the 'loss of experience' produced through market reification and through encountering the big city and the crowd. The 'fanciful fencing' of the rhymer, the duel with beauty in which the artist 'cries out in fright before being vanquished' and the anxiety of the poet 'elbowed' by the crowd, supposedly translate a modern experience of shock in which the worker's automatism in being riveted to his machine, the pedestrian's anxiety at each inter-section, the gambler's attention to every dice throw and the camera's click all participate equally. And it is with relation to the inorganic power that gives its law to experience, or rather to the modern loss thereof – i.e. the reified fetish of the commodity

– that we must supposedly understand the flaneur's intoxication, his enjoying being like a commodity 'tossed about in the stream of clients'; the enigmatic enjoyment of number that becomes clear 'if one imagines it spoken not from the point of view of the human, but also from that of the commodity'[7]; and finally the destructive rage of the allegory, interrupting the course of history to stamp the reified world with the emblem of the only 'radical novelty' still available – death.

This interpretative gesture, which reads in the words and cadences of the poem the heroic transcription of a devastated sensory experience, cuts perhaps a little too fast through the aesthetic fabric within which the Baudelairian reverie of the infinite Republic becomes meaningful. It swings over to the viewpoint of a 'destruction of experience' something that is much rather a modification in the system of relations between elements defining a form of experience: ways of being and doing, seeing, thinking and saying. To avoid this short-circuit, it is useful to reinscribe the Baudelairian experience of the city and the crowd within the larger set of transformations that affected the poetic paradigm in his time.

It is perhaps from this point of view that we might re-examine the theme of the 'heroism of modern life'. Those who have underlined the importance in Baudelaire of the theme of heroism and its embodiment in the 'modern' figure of the dandy have scarcely afforded any attention to certain singular

occurrences of the term in his texts. In the preface to his translation of Poe, Baudelaire inserts some emphatic praise for savage
nations, happily deprived of the 'ingenious inventions that
exempt the individual from heroism', whereas the civilized man
finds himself confined 'in the infinitely small region of speci-
ality'.[8] The savage is at once warrior and poet. With his clothing,
his ornaments and his weapons, he even makes for the perfect
figure of the dandy, a 'supreme embodiment of the idea of the
beautiful in material life'.[9] This identification is reprised in the
Salon de 1859 in which the tribal chiefs painted by Fromentin
make clear to the eyes of the critic the same 'Patrician dandyism'
as the American Indians George Catlin once painted and who,
'even in their state of fall, make us dream of the art of Phidias
and of Homeric grandeurs'.[10] The features of modern heroism
and of Baudelairian dandyism thus come very close to those
of Schillerian 'naïve poetry' and aesthetic education. Heroism
is not primarily the virtue of individuals. It is the virtue of the
world that brings together the reasons for acting and those of
the poem. A hero is not a fearless man who engages in dazzling
feats. He is the inhabitant of an intermediary world between
the human and the divine. This mediation between separated
worlds makes poetry possible. But the hero is also the being who
knows no separation between the orders of acting and doing.
This was how Hegel described the heroic universe specific to
Homeric poetry: a world that ignores the division of labour, in

which princes and warlords cut their meat themselves and are able to carve their own beds or forge their own weapons. The condition of naïve or heroic poetry is that the world is already poetic; and it is so by virtue of that indistinction from which Hegel regards the modern world of science, the economy and rational administration as definitively removed.

To this verdict, the era of Balzac and Dumas, we know, already replied: the condition of 'naïve' indistinction can be rediscovered as much on the streets of the modern metropolis as on the trail of Fenimore Cooper's Indians. Modernity also has its heroism, i.e. its poeticity able to be read directly in the decor of the city, the manners and gait of its inhabitants, as well as in the gaping abysses in its depths below or behind its portes-cochères, and that set the world of the ordinary in communication with the universe of the fantastic. The novelist or poet is the observer – half-flaneur at the lookout for the picturesque in human mores, half-clairvoyant plumbing the gaping abysses beneath one's feet or behind walls – who exhumes the poetry immanent to the prosaic world: the special and fleeting beauty, 'modern' in a word, that comes, according to Baudelaire, to be added to the eternal element of art. But finding virgin forests and Mohicans in Paris is only the simplest part of the programme. 'Naïve' poetry was not the picturesque poetry of mores of yesteryear, and one must not be taken in by the *trompe-l'œil* produced by the literature of 'physiologies', which were all the rage around

1840. The physiological project seems primarily to summon the entomologist's gaze, as he analyses the ethos proper to each social type. But the author of physiologies, most often, does not observe anything at all. He threads commonplaces whose assemblage emblematizes a type. The matter is trifling since this encyclopedic pseudo-knowledge on society serves no purpose, since it is not a form of knowledge able to arm those who pursue social ends.

That is precisely the crux of the problem. The heroic world was the world of indistinction between the poetic sphere and that of action. And this very indistinction is what appears lost. Balzac, who, far more than Poe, forged the Baudelairian gaze on the city and the crowd, provided the most brilliant illustration of it. The minutely detailed and hallucinatory description that begins *The Girl with the Golden Eyes* of the five circles of Parisian hell emerged as the masterwork of a new novelistic ethology. But this ethology in no way contributes to the fictional energy that supplies the novel with its action. Moreover, the penetrative ability of the Thirteen is perfectly powerless to halt the disaster. Having knowledge of the multiplicity of social identities as well as of the turns, detours and abysses of the big city can serve to remythologize the world. But it does so only at the price of more firmly dismissing the lost paradise of the heroic world, as a world of immediate union between manners of being and manners of acting. To give full meaning to the poet's resentment concerning a world 'in which action is not the sister of dream',[11] it must be inscribed within the logic of a much more radical rupture. It is not dream that breaks with action. Instead, the promotion of dream results from the divorce accomplished between knowledge and action.

From the procrastinations of General Wallenstein to the wanderings of Wilhelm Meister, including the failed ventures of Balzac's conspirators, the absurd gunshot of Julien Sorel, the fatigue of Büchner's Danton, the idleness of Frédéric Moreau and the illusions of Tolstoy's generals, the entire era named romantic seems, in fact, to be haunted in its plots and affected in its forms of construction by a single obsession: the failure of action. Action, as is well known, is not simply the fact of doing something. It is a mode of thought, a structure of rationality that defines both a norm of legitimate social behaviours and a norm of composition of fictions. Such was the Aristotelian arranging of actions linked through bonds of causality according to necessity or verisimilitude. The rationality of action corresponds to a certain form of the whole: that constituted by a denumerable and coherent set of relations – relations of coordination between causes and effects, of subordination between centre and periphery. Action requires a finite world, circumscribed knowledge, calculable forms of causality and designated actors. Now, this limitation appears lost to Balzac's contemporaries and successors. The problem is not that the world has become too prosaic for elite souls to find satisfaction in it. It is that it has become too vast, and that knowledge has become too subtle, too differentiated for action to be able to find in it the suitable conditions of rarity. When aiming to designate the vice of new fiction, to which *L'Éducation sentimentale* bears witness, Barbey d'Aurevilly invokes the authority not of a literary man but of a general, Napoléon Bonaparte. The latter supposedly had reproached his brother Joseph for having 'a terrible fault that prevents all action [ ] *the kind of imagination* that, above all, *fills the head with pictures*'.[12] To fill one's head with pictures is to impede the field of action, render its lines confused and its very goals derisory. Now, new social science itself does not stop making 'pictures' that widen the distance between thought and action. In these conditions, the search for the contemporary world's own specific form of 'heroization' appears torn between two poles. On the one hand, heroic unity will be sought in a radicalization of the principle of voluntary action, in the pure decision to act, with or without ground. On the other, it will be found on the sole side of reverie, which cancels out the distortions that the will imprints on the course of things and enables the spectacle of modern life to unfold all its virtualities.

Baudelaire initially appears to take the former option. Discovering Poe and his 'poetic principle' permits him to fix the image of the poet who does exactly as he had projected and leaves behind no word that would not be the effect of an intention. But it also leads the author who seeks to test himself by writing novels or five-act plays to a strange observation: this poetic unity, formerly associated with the grand forms of tragedy and epic, now obliges one to limit oneself to the small forms of which the novella is the model. Such are the means, vouchsafes the poet, that make it possible to obtain the desired effect, i.e. unity of impression, via absolute control over all elements of the poem. But this strategic rationalization does a poor job at hiding the change in the very nature of the poetic: the 'totality' to be aimed at now is that 'excitation' of soul, which, 'of psychological necessity', is fugitive and transitory.[13] That is the crux of the problem: the totality that gives its norm to the poem is no longer the organic body with well-coordinated, functional limbs. Baudelaire's cadet, Hippolyte Taine, will hammer it home ceaselessly: the old beauty was that of bodies with muscles tensed for action. The modern age, as for it, is that of the nervous man. Benjamin sought to tie this theme of nervousness, which becomes an obsession in Baudelaire's era, to that of shock, which he sees at the heart of the experience of the city and crowds. And, likewise, he linked the destruction of the organic model to the inorganic power of the commodity and the cadaver. But the refutation of the organic model is not the triumph of the inorganic. Opposed to the organism is not the inorganic; it is life as power that circulates through bodies, exceeds their limits and disorganizes the relation itself of thought to its effect. In fact, the effect that Baudelaire attributes to hashish ought to be generalized to the new set of perceptive experiences: all loss of 'equivalence between the organs and pleasures'.[14] The science of mind being established at the time parallels in this regard the science of society. Both explode what they were initially supposed to complete: the model of the organism, of the centre that commands it, the muscles that tense and the limbs that obey. The finite world of the organism – which is also one of action – now finds itself exceeded on two sides: on the side of its theatre, which no longer provides circumscribed scenes for action, and on the side of its agent, whose temporality no longer happens to coincide with the source of that action. The social world is lost in infinite ramifications. And similarly for the subject that was the cause of action. Its identity gets lost in the infinite smallness of sensations. The unity of the poem is a unity of effect and this latter has to correspond to a short excitation. The masterpiece of programmatic will thus comes very close to the conjuring trick of the illusionist or the charlatan. Will is no longer the rational adjustment of means to desired ends; it is essentially the act of its self-exhibition. And this is never so pure as when it is groundless, as when it is identified with the pure nervous discharge inflicted on the bad glazier, as he is hurled from the top of the staircase with his glass panes.

These displays and caricatures of the will are unable to re-establish any 'heroic' unity. Here again the art critic's gaze belies the boastfulness of the poet, master of his effects: 'In art one thing is not sufficiently noted, the share reserved for the will of man is not nearly as large as is thought.'[15] If the new poetic form has to be brief, it is not to vouchsafe the mastery of the artist. It is, on the contrary, because it marks the punctual encounter between a subject, who is an infinite network of sensations, and a sensible world that exceeds all closure of the field of strategic action. The unity of the poem is that of the 'patch of sky seen through the basement window', giving 'a more profound idea of the infinite than the panorama seen from a mountain peak',[16] just as that of a painting is 'that dusty and luminous atmosphere of a room into which the sun wants to enter fully'.[17] The world exceeds the field of action just as the subject exceeds the circle of the will. The act of thought that takes this excess into account bears a name; it is called reverie. Reverie is not the withdrawal into the inner world of one who no longer wants to act because reality has disappointed him. It is not the contrary of action but another mode of thought, another mode of the rationality of things. It is not the refusal of external reality but the mode of thought that calls into question the very boundary that the organic model imposed between 'inner' reality, where thought decided, and 'external' reality, in which it produced its effects.

It is here that the gaze upon the city and the urban experience become meaningful. In order to grasp this, it is necessary to relativize the radical novelty that Walter Benjamin, in order to make it coincide with the age of industrial capitalism and commodity fetishism, attributes to the urban experience of Baudelaire's contemporaries. This urban experience is not that of curious *flanerie*, which instead belongs to the age of Sébastien Mercier and Rétif de la Bretonne. Nor is it that of the traumatizing crowd. And it is probably necessary to limit the importance given to Edgar Poe and his 'man of the crowd', which the Benjaminian reading privileges because this man's journey ends up at sites of the commodity and crime. Baudelaire borrowed the model for his gaze upon the city less from Poe than from Balzac. Not Balzac the geologist of circles of the big city and observer of the types that stride along its boulevards, of their gait or their habits, but the Balzac who experienced the inanity of that physiological or physiognomic knowledge and fictionalized the very gap between knowledge about society and the success of action. Exemplary from this point of view is the last episode of *Ferragus*, in which the inconsolable spouse stops his carriage at the city limits, close to the ill-defined grounds of the Observatory where the bowls players meet. No physiology is given of this picturesque urban character. The voyeur's gaze is cast on another spectator: the former plot leader of the Thirteen conspirators out to conquer society now become the inert observer of this game of bowls, or, as Balzac says in an expression that sounds like a dream title for a prose poem, 'the fantastic genius of the jack ball'.[18]

Baudelaire's first reflection on the heroism of modern life refers, as is well known, to Balzac. In it, Baudelaire couples the 'spectacle of fashionable life' with that of 'millions of floating existences that circulate in the underground passages of a big city'.[19] The relation between the modern, the heroic and the floating is worth dwelling on. In fact, this is the fullest sense of the otherwise banal statement according to which the beautiful is made of an eternal element and a fleeting element tied to the present. It is not simply a matter of combining today's beauty with the beauty of old. It is a matter of identifying a specifically modern beauty, in contrast with classical beauty – enemy to 'line-shifting movement' – a beauty of the 'floating', that is to say, precisely, of the erased line. Floating existences are, in fact, much more than the 'criminals and kept women' Baudelaire mentions – thinking perhaps of Vautrin and Esther. These existences are not definable by the features of intermediary classes or populations of interlopers. They are definable simply by their belonging to a floating world. This world does not simply consist in the non-stop traffic of big cities. It is above all a world without stable base, definable circumference or well-established identities. Instead of identifying it with a specific social fauna – bohemian or other – of which Baudelaire would be the representative, this 'flotation' must be given its aesthetic dimension. The floating world is a world in which the lines of division between social identities are blurred; likewise, in Delacroix's

painting the line – both framework and emblem of the representational order – comes to be eliminated twice over: according to
the truth of geometers, for whom each one contains a thousand
of them, and that of the colourists, for whom it is only ever 'the
intimate merging of two colours'.[20]

This is the model through which the experience of the crowd
must be grasped. It is primarily a model of the experience of a
dreamer. The Baudelairian observer does not embark, as does
Poe's, in pursuit of characters who have struck his gaze, not
even the passing woman that he might have loved.[21] To follow
her would be to denude her of what made her aura, namely not
some apparition of the distant or some death blow, but very
simply the past conditional as the mode and tense of the *fugitive,*
mode and time of an appearing that is not merely ephemeral
but is above all divested of the properties that render so prosaic
any 'dear soul' from the moment it has consented to follow you.
The model of the Baudelairian voyeur is the man who looks
at the crowd from afar and on high, in a gaze that renders the
latter indistinct. It is the dreamer behind his window, observing
'beyond the waves/oceans of roofs', such and such of those black
or luminous holes in which 'life lives, life dreams, life suffers'.[22]
Balzac again provides the model with Raphaël from *La peau
de chagrin* who, from his garret, casts his gaze over those 'Paris
savannahs formed by roofs, flat as a plain but covering populous
abysses';[23] and also the Victor Hugo of *La pente de la rêverie,*

who sees through gothic windows familiar faces lose their
features as they melt into an immense crowd that extends across
continents, deserts and oceans:

> Nameless crowd! steps, voices, eyes – a chaos!
> Those who have never yet been seen or known.[24]

> *Foule sans nom! Chaos! Des voix, des yeux, des pas.*
> *Ceux qu'on n'a jamais vus, ceux qu'on ne connaît pas.*

The beauty the urban dreamer grasps is not that of the fashion
of the day. Nor is it that of death perceived through the eternal
repetition of the new. The rotting carcass is not the emblem of
the vanity of all beauty; it itself offers a singular beauty, that
of the multiple buzzing of flies and maggots, and of forms
that erase themselves until they are no more than a dream,
a forgotten 'sketch' on a painter's canvas.[25] Modern beauty is
not the 'always the same' Benjamin that obsessed over after
his reading of Blanqui and that he saw emblematized in the
phantasmagoria of Baudelaire's *Sept vieillards*. On the contrary,
modern beauty is that of the anonymous multiple, of the body
that has lost the lines that enclosed it, of the being denuded of
its identity. But this loss of identity must not itself get lost in the
sonorous chaos of Hugolian pantheism. Universal life is not the
ocean into which all sinks. It is necessary to give to the multiple
and to enjoyment of the multiple a framework that prevents

them from getting lost in the deafening murmur of the crowd/ ocean and in compassion for the woes of the world. Serving this is the window that shows and hides, the encounter with singular beings whose faces bear a history but, since Balzac, have lost the power to tell it and the exchange of gazes that opens an infinite vanishing line in the everyday space of the city. It is important that the window first and foremost opens only onto a world of other windows, behind which stands, for example, that wrinkly woman leaning over something indefinable and whose face, clothing and confused gesture permit a story to be made up.[26] Modern beauty is also this: no longer a way of inventing stories that stage scenes with characters similar to us, but instead of making oneself dissimilar by inventing the possible lives of real beings glimpsed behind a casement window or at a bend in the street. And this, notably, is what permits the 'sinuous' aspect of the prose poem, in which all is both head and tail. Behind the offhandedness of the comments that preface *Le Spleen de Paris* there is a complete redefinition of poetic mimesis, to which the dreamlike form of the prose poem lends itself.

Its freedom consists in far more than the replacing of regular metre by the convenience of the sinuous line. It participates in the ruining of an entire tradition of thinking about the poem. Long ago Aristotle redeemed mimesis from Plato's attacks by shifting away it from the imitation of characters toward the composition of those actions that distinguish themselves from the ordinariness of life because they have a head and a tail, a beginning, a middle and an end. With the loss of the paradigm of action, mimesis again comes to be the invention of characters. But this new mimesis inverts the old logic according to which the poet would invent beings of fiction to whose feelings actors lent their real bodies. Henceforth, real bodies must rather serve as supports for the creations of reverie, on the condition, of course, of being stripped of their properties, and rendered available for reverie to reinhabit them. Such is ultimately the moral – *à tiroirs* – of *Le vieux saltimbanque*. The poem seems entirely devoted to celebrating this new beauty, which is placed under the egalitarian sign of the effervescence of the multiple, wherein gain and loss make one 'equally joyful' about the fete, and wherein, as in a Decamps painting, all is merely 'light, dust, cries, joy, tumult'.[27] And the very perfection of the painting is what appears is contributed by the encounter of the old entertainer leaning against the posts of his shack, like Ferragus against his tree, but whose gaze, instead of setting itself on the path of the bowls, wanders 'profound, unforgettable' around the changing flux of the crowd and the light. The reader thus begrudges the poet for ending his walk with the dullest of allegories: the old entertainer provides the image of the 'old man of letters who has outlived the generation he so brilliantly amused'.[28] But this very dull conclusion can in turn be unfolded and made to reverberate on the urban stroll. The old man of letters, whose shack is empty, is also the poet fixed to his identity, playing the role of the poet. The multiple life and the multiple lives in which the new poet must lose himself releases him from that outmoded role. The profound gaze of the old entertainer therefore stands not as the contrary of the poetry of the multiple but instead is its multiplier. More exactly it opens in the simple multiplicity of the crowd the line of an infinitization. The crowd does not merely present bodies available for the modern poet's embodiments. It also presents singular encounters, gazes that cause to deviate the very enjoyment that they increase and which prevent it from closing again into possession. The wealthy man's joy is miserly when it has not been infinitized by the poor man's gaze, stretched toward the café's lights and decorations, or by his ear, which strains to hear the distant echoes of the concert; but the poor man's joy remains petty, too, so long as it has not been traversed by the gaze of one who no longer has anything to show to onlookers. It is this republican infinitization of sensation that those 'dear souls' cannot understand, since their satisfied consumption refuses to be spoiled by poor people with eyes 'as wide open as portes-cochères'.[29] The enjoyment of the multiple is unable to become enclosed either in solitary possession or in amorous reciprocity. Poetic 'prostitution' is decidedly something other than the emblematic exhibition of that commodity in which life is made a symbol of death. And the infinitization of the multiple is not contradictory with the rejection of progress.

The poet, who laughed of his past revolutionary extravagances, remained steadfast on this point: 'It is a good thing sometimes to teach the fortunate of this world, if only to humble for an instant their stupid pride, that there are higher joys than theirs, more vast, more refined.'[30] The unknown is not merely the chasm at the bottom of which death is the only assured novelty. Behind each window, at the crossing of each street, at the threshold of each place of pleasure, it can offer itself to the aesthetic Republic's work of infinitization. It is a modest but faithful politics. The issue is not to reduce to this alone the entire work and thought of a poet who had multiple faces and roles. But taking it into account can help us to cast a new gaze on this very multiplicity and reopen the space specific to the unfolding of its contradictory virtualities. The problem, moreover, is not one about interpreting a poet. It is to grasp the mutations of gaze and thought, the divisions of time and space, of words and images, according to which the idea of poetry and the Republic combined to draw a certain visage of community.

6

The theatre of thoughts

What occurred in modern theatre between thought, speech and action, and especially in the theatre practice that laid claim to renewing with 'the people' a link pertaining to theatre's very essence? I shall raise this question on the basis of a personal recollection. One evening in early 1954, I descended the large staircase of the Palais de Chaillot for my first encounter with Jean Vilar's *Théâtre national populaire*. Whoever had discovered theatre through their subscription to the Comédie-Française was obviously going to be in for a shock. Awaiting the spectator was a huge and bare stage, bereft of curtain. Sitting anywhere in front of it you were sure to get a good view of everything, regardless of how much you had paid for your ticket. Instead of the bell urging people to take their seats, there were trumpets, and instead of three blows and the curtain raise, a simple moment in the dark before the light returned to the bare stage, whereupon some colour blotches of flags moved about. This entry into the play served as a sort of warning to the audience, notifying it that something other than social entertainment was about to take place on the open space of the stage: the spectacle of a certain grandeur, one belonging to the heroic essence of theatre and forming an intermediary between the audience gathered there and the on-stage movements being exhibited – in the case at hand, the movements of a Shakespearean drama linked to some of History's memorable events.

Concerning this story of flags and fanfares, one moment remains engraved in my mind, namely when the actor who portrayed Richard II – and who at this time was also the embodiment of radiant beauty and generous youth – addressed the last of those still faithful to the monarch in these terms: 'My friends, let us sit down on the ground and recount the lamentable end of the kings.' At that moment, the large space available for the action's unfolding and for the resonance of words shrunk to this small circle of discussants, who let the action simply play on, abandoning it to itself. The matter was indeed about the end of a king, and the history of peoples primarily comprises the decline of kings. But this dissociation between the small-circle conversation and the story's action, left to run by itself, and which the circle remained content to comment upon, also marked the destiny of the revolutionaries that, not long before, this same theatre had staged with *Dantons Tod,* or with the story of a political murder committed without reason in *Lorenzaccio.* And not long after it was to stage, with *Platonov*, the endless gossiping of a provincial Russia commenting on its own stasis, which, outside of a gunshot – whose doer had to have two cracks at it – is interrupted only through the vertiginous gap created between two phrases of a farewell letter: 'Love our little Kolya as I love him. Watch over my brother. Do not abandon our father. *Live according to the Scriptures. The key to the chest-of-drawers is in my woollen dress.*'[1]

How are we to conceive this breakdown of action and this loss of connection between phrases that became manifest on the enlarged stage of the people's theatre? Some fifty years later, I read the diagnosis given of it at the time by another spectator, whom this performance of Richard II, which I had found enchanting, had left feeling exasperated. In the performance of Gérard Philippe, Barthes saw the sign of the fatal embourgeoisement of the people's theatre.[2] I will revisit this diagnosis and the politics of the theatre it entails. But the problem no doubt came from further away. Behind the possible 'embourgeoisement' of an initiative of people's theatre initiative in the 1950s, there is an originary tension that inhabits the system of thought concerning theatrical action, within which this project had its scene of deployment. For, from its beginnings the notion of a people's theatre encountered a radical questioning of what theatre could mean as a relation between thoughts, speech and acts.

To understand it, let us set out from the historical moment when this idea of a people's theatre was formulated, an idea that was being played out on the stage of the Palais de Chaillot. Victor Hugo, in his 1833 preface to *Marie Tudor* – another play performed by Jean Vilar's TNP – formulated its principle: that of the enlarged stage on which romantic poetics, demolishing the conventions of the classical order, came to coincide with a political stage, which had hitherto been foreign and even hostile to it, namely that of the sovereign people, recently rejuvenated by the revolution of July 1830. The theatre stage came to be enlarged not merely by destroying the genres and proprieties linked to it, but also by exceeding the limited viewpoints according to which the major classics had selected their characters and situations and decided upon the passionate motivations of their plots. New drama was to consist in 'the mix on the stage of all that is involved in life; [it was to consist] in a riot here and a talk about love there, and within the talk about love, a lesson for the people, and within the riot, a cry of the heart; [it was to consist] in the laugh; in tears; in good, evil, the high and the low, fatality, providence, genius, chance, society, the world, nature, life; and above all this one would feel something great hovering.'[3] To match the new people of revolutionary days, Hugo was to propose the radical egalitarianism of that enlarged stage. Its model, of course, is Shakespearian dramaturgy: the stage of the historical drama in which the movement of great human interests carries with it the particular interests and passions of princes; in which the rule of unities is lost, enabling action to distend into episodes of diverse intensity and coloration; where life is thus present in its entire truth, under all its aspects, serious, comical or indifferent. Its difference was simply that the common people, who in Shakespeare were doomed to comic uses, now gained, with Didier, Gilbert or Ruy Blas, great heroic roles. Further, however, what perforce appears in the people's theatre is not the people but instead something greater than it – Humanity. And what manifests itself on that great stage of Humanity is, in turn, a power larger than Humanity. This power, twice named in our extract, is called Life, the universal Life that traverses and exceeds the lives of individuals.

Life is what turns the stage into the site of a new dramaturgy, a dramaturgy of coexistence. Still, the forms of this dramaturgy require thinking through, that is, the new articulation it implies between the powers in play at theatre: thoughts, speech and actions. Victor Hugo's reflection seems to stop at this point. For him, to enable life to flow, it seemed sufficient to abolish the old properties of characters, situations and language. But life is not simply the flow that unfolds freely once all hindrances have been lifted. As a dramaturgical principle, it requires a redistribution of the play of these 'hindered' powers. And here we find the core of the problem: theatre is not simply the metaphor of a social order. It is also a metaphor of thought. Now, hitherto, there had been two great figures of the relation between thought and theatre. There was the negative model of the Platonic cave, in which theatre appears as thought's contrary, that is, the reign of the image, which is to say: the lie of the poet, hidden behind personages, and of the actor, who plays at being that which he is not; the passivity and illusion of the spectators who see paraded and take as truth the shadows whose mechanism of production they are ignorant of; the enjoyment that they take in the spectacle of these ignorant and ill personages, created and embodied by liars; the handclapping of the great popular animal; and the evil of excessiveness, which is introduced into souls, through the spectacle of passion that leaves sensible traces in them.

There is that negative model. And there is the positive model set down in Aristotle's *Poetics,* in which dramatic action is, conversely, a model of thought in act: the construction of a plot as the linking of actions in line with necessity and verisimilitude. In this case, drama is a model of rationality, an arrangement of causes and effects that has the spectator take part in a plot of knowledge. This model is, we know, given through a certain play of similitudes and oppositions. To the simple succession of things that happen one after another, it contrasts the linking of events whereby time is determined by relations of causality: ones that depend on characters' calculations and others that link their actions together in spite of themselves. This model of unity of events that are subjected to a causal law also receives expression in an analogy, that of the organism in which members are coordinated and subjected to a centre. The visible space of representation is thus presented as the site of effectuation of a wholly intellectual schema, an assembling of actions that is expressed through a joust of discourse. Of course this abstract site of an intellectual process was also, in the classical age, the very concrete site in which men who were supposedly expert in the art of speaking and of acting through speech took pleasure in the on-stage representation of that power. And the question of 'people's' theatre arose when this supposedly natural circle came to be broken between actors and spectators equally expert in the art of speech that acts. But the important thing, for the image of thought, is the submission of the space of representation to the time of dramatic action, a time determined as the assemblage of actions driven entirely by speech – which presupposes a twofold tie of speech: to the source of thought and of will that it expresses; and to the effect that it produces in terms of action.

The problem of new drama, then, is to know what rupture its dramaturgy operates with relation to this twofold image of thought: thought as subjugated to the parade of images and thought as active in the self-sufficient formation of a causal plot. What does this life, which is its key word, imply as a new form of rationality? What relations does this rationality entertain with the models of causality of action and of organic harmony of parts? What mode of thought's efficacy plays out in the drama's progression? What role does speech play in it? What are the functions of space and time in it? These questions scarcely concerned the inventor of a 'national' and 'people's' theatre. However, they did preoccupy the mind of a young man tasked with translating *Marie Tudor* into German, namely Georg Büchner. Büchner no doubt echoed the author he had translated, notably in the famous tirade given to Camille Desmoulins in *Dantons Tod*: what up to then passed for theatrical truths were merely marionettes that embodied an idea and a hint of feeling. What is to be done, says Camille, is to go into the streets and set down to the school of exuberant Creation. But the following problem immediately arises: this exuberant creation has in actual fact never been created. It has neither beginning nor end. Well, a piece of theatre has the minimum requisite of having to have a beginning, an end and also a middle, that is to say, a vehicle that regulates the path of this beginning to this end. But life is also a middle [or milieu] in a new sense, not as the interval between two extremes, but as a fabric in which everything is interwoven to infinity, so much so that one never finds oneself at the point where the cause begins to act and nowhere can one determine the point at which its effect stops.

This is uttered in the first lines of the *Dantons Tod*, in which the apparently rambling conversation ceaselessly mixes into the action a reflection on what action may henceforth mean. Since the organic model that governed the image of dramatic action and of living discourse is henceforth obsolete. The model of the living is now the nervous system, an endless network of fibres and synapses that permit of no enclosure within the unity of an organism or of mobilization within the unity of an action. Summing this up, in the first scene, is Danton's quip, made in reply to Camille, who presses him to act: 'In one hour's time, sixty minutes will have passed.' 'So what? That stands to reason', replies Camille.[4] But behind that truism lies not merely Zeno's old paradox. What the quip implies is that the time of action is eaten up by an infinite regression toward the question of its point of departure. The problem, then, is not simply to seize the – impossible to locate – moment of beginning, but instead to grasp the point where *that* begins. It is to know *who* or *what* effectuates this beginning.

The clarification of Danton's quip – Danton himself does not act or acts only to 'kill time' – is reserved for his adversary, Robespierre, the one who acts, in a scene that is like an echo of Macbeth's hallucinatory meditation before the crime weapon: 'Some part of me, I don't know which, contradicts the rest … Thoughts, desires, hardly dreamt of, confused and formless, which shuddered away from the daylight, now take shape and crawl into the silent house of dreams. They open doors, look out of windows, they half become flesh. Limbs stretch in sleep, lips mutter. And isn't waking consciousness only a clearer dream? Are we not sleepwalkers? Are not our actions dream actions, only more sharply defined, more complete? Who will blame us for that? The mind performs more thinking acts in an hour than this sluggish organism, the body, can imitate in years. Sin is in the mind. Whether thought becomes action, whether the body carries it out, is mere chance.'[5]

Here Danton's quip receives its profound meaning. The hour does not simply divide into an infinity of instants. It decomposes into an infinity of thoughts, whose rhythm no act can follow, and whose provenance no mind can master, determine the justice of or decide by itself the means of realization. No thought has any reason to wait for its act. That does not mean that it will not act but that it will act only as thought that does not know itself: either spectre or hallucination. Saint-Just does his best to rationalize matters: the moral revolution, he says, must employ, if it is to be carried out, the same destructive paths as revolutions of the globe. But the rhetorical argument is unable to hide the crack at the core of thought's new image – an image that theatre portrays but that is also henceforth theatre's own law: thought acts inasmuch as it is an unmasterable territory, a territory on which one knows not whence ideas come, and where these latter act only in the mode of the dream or sleepwalking. Thought is excess, excess over acts, excess over itself. So thought's effect itself can only be excessive: it escapes the mastery of individuals engaged in pursuing ends and determining the means to arrive at them; and it is foreign to the normal relations that determine which causes produce which effects.

The sleepwalker ritual of the 1793 Revolution thus answers to the scene in which the people appear in broad daylight during the days of July 1830, just as the Macbeths' visions and halluci-nations answer to the dream of Victor Hugo's grand unanimist theatre. The enlarged stage of the Shakespearean drama shrinks to a fundamental conflict: the conflict, on the one hand, between the lazy, between those who, like Hamlet and Danton, follow the indolence of the flesh because they have no reason to institute moments when the action would start; and, on the other, the sleepwalkers, those who, like Macbeth and Robespierre, grant that thought shakes up this indolence by taking flesh in its manner and producing from it its own autonomous effects, according to the logic of the waking dream. Thus shattered is the old opposition that structured the idea of theatrical rationality, the opposition of poetic action that forms a whole of thought and of the pure succession of facts that occur one after the other. Thought is not the unity of the multiple that contrasts with the isolated succession of facts. It is itself the 'disordered' succession of 'facts of thought'. And the acts that this succession determines have as many reasons to be as not to be. The model for this is given with the great Shakespearean murderers, but also with the 'fait divers', which establishes itself as a new model of novelistic narration or the stage plot right when the people is taking to the streets of Paris and when the French poet is dreaming of the great stage of coexistence of everything with everything.

The *fait divers*, in fact, is the isolated act, in which is deployed a power of acting that breaks with the supposedly normal course of life 'without history'. It is the act that, in a sense, is reduced to itself, subtracted from the causal chains according to which the state of things is reproduced. But is it also an act that, by the same token, opens onto a new type of narration and interpretation: one that sees directly encapsulated in the singularity of the act the law of a whole that is no longer an organism whose members would have to be reconstituted, but instead a reticular system in which each moment in some way bears the power of the whole. This contourless whole may be the state of society in which the act thus becomes the symptom. Soldier Woyzeck's murderous act attests outright, without mediations, to the humiliated human condition with which a society afflicts common people, as well as to the violence with which they respond to it. But it also brings to light the way that the great network of obscure forces, thoughts and personal images gets individualized as the thought and act of an individual, whether this latter be a prince or a simple soldier. This act can therefore no longer be inscribed within the Aristotelian logic of peripeteia and recognition. It is merely the term of a chain of some dreamy or nightmarish visions: the champignons that grow in patterns on the ground, the noise of violins, the sparkle of a pair of earrings, a blade seen first during sleep, a red colour which is that of the moon's rising before being the effect of knife blows: a series of acts identical to a chain of thoughts, itself the same as a parade of nocturnal visions opening doors or looking through windows.

This translator thus reverses the Hugolian dream of a theatre of universal life coincident with the people's appearing on history's stage, is thus reversed by this translator, who transposed it in terms of an image of thought and seized it in a stranglehold between his physiologist's scalpel and his experience as a republican militant – witness to the failure of volontarism on the part of those who believed that taking over a guardroom in Frankfurt was enough to provoke the German people into uprising.[6] But merely contrasting the helping hand of mindless activists with the patience of the historical process is not enough. *Danton's Death* also proclaims thought's ruin as a rational historical unfolding, which the Aristotelian rationality of the poem, composed according to necessity or verisimilitude, had wanted to transfer onto the course of successive events. The strategy of the 1793 revolutionaries produces its effects no differently to the delirium of the soldier Woyzeck, with his knife before him, at once real and dreamt, as Macbeth had his before him, or Robespierre the lists that Saint-Just presented him. Opposite activist infantilism stands only the great blanket of thoughts and desires, issuing from who knows which depths, that similarly people the vigil of the advocate of Arras and the dreams of the imbecilic soldier, that marry the words and refrain of a popular song or are heroized into a national hymn, that take flesh like a knife cut or a guillotine blade.

— Thus, on the stage of the people's theatre, the gap seems to institute itself from the outset. Instead of being a space of young popular energies and the great human family, its enlarged space is one of spectres, of those who obey their orders and those who sit down on the ground to watch the effects of this flit by. The affair does not shrink to the disenchantment of the revolutionary, who is just in too much of a rush to see thought ignite the 'naïve popular terrain' not to transform the first failure into the radical conclusion that this thought will never affect the uncouth body of the people, unless in the mode of sleepwalking action. It marks an irremediable gap with the conception of causality that bolstered both classical plot construction and the forms of revolutionary action. The reticular interlacing of manifestations of life, the evasion of the point of departure, the law of the middle with neither beginning nor end and the uncertain zone where shadow mixes with clear thought – all that will also come to impose itself on whoever seeks to ground in the science of society the means to innovate with relation to the lapsed schemas of programmed action. The consequences of this go beyond the limits of my remarks, which seek only to grasp the constitution of a thought of theatre, one that is at once an image of thought and a form of interpretation of the paths and effects of action, and thus also a form of interpretation of society and history. At issue is to see how this theatre of thought has been able to take body as an effective theatre and to impose the framework of this effective theatre upon desires to place 'the people' before the image of its greatness.

To see it, then, we must set out again from the question raised above: what operation is performed by the new thought of the enlarged drama, and by the paradigm of life that governs it, with relation to the two models of the theatre as place of mendacious images and as positive plot of knowledge? Bluntly stated, the reply is expressed as follows: the theatre of well-constructed actions, of speech that sums up thought and leads it to act – all that which claimed to contrast with the shadow of marionettes projected on the cave wall – was itself but a theatre of marionettes, giving a bodily device to abstract ideas. It is dramatic action as the plot of knowledge that is a lie: one about the nature of thought and the way in which it takes shape and is acted out; about the motivations and paths of action. The truth is the positive efficacy of shadows, is the non-knowledge of what is at the origin of thoughts and actions, is the impossibility of determining the relation between the succession of states and the chain of causes and effects, and is the equal possibility that the act either is or is not produced. It is, in short, the collapse of the entire logic of verisimilitude in favour of the immediate identity between the power of the true and the power of shadows. This refutation of the plot of knowledge clearly does not mark a return to the image of the cave. For this latter presumes the existence of a site from which one can see both the effective light of truth and the puppet-master who produces the shadows. Well, no such place exists and there is no puppet-master other than life itself. Life is truth given in the form of a theatre of shadows. Theatre thus becomes an exemplary site to see not truth but its effects, and to make visible, through the play of these effects, the lie of the model of mastered action.

The structure – theoretical and practical – of this place is thus necessarily paradoxical. What there is that is worth presenting at the theatre is life, life in its truth, which from everywhere overflows the limits of the functional organism and end-driven actions. Life is not recounted in discourse; it has to manifest itself perceptibly. But this manifestation immediately encounters its contradiction. For true life, precisely, evades manifest perception. Life is thoughts, no longer as the expression of the intentions of personages, but as phantoms that come to haunt their brains, like visions the spectators do not see – we are no longer in the era of witches – but whose power they are to experience. Life is words, which are no longer there to announce or tell of actions, but instead to make felt the content of a sensible milieu, to enable perception of the unsaid that haunts them and which is expressed only by the silence separating them. The stage must show the invisible dimension from which come, and to which are to be lost, the thoughts and act of which it is the place. Theatre is henceforth the place that has to render sensible its out-place (*hors-lieu*), which has to show its being inhabited, its being structured, with respect to this out-place. It has to be fashioned by its relation to the invisible dimension surrounding it, through the partitions, doors and windows across which the unknown takes effect. This is what the playwright and theoretician of theatre, Maurice Maeterlinck, theorized under the name of motionless theatre: a theatre where the reasons for moving are indistinguishable from those for not moving.

This structure is one he came to present at least once in all its literality. I am thinking of his play in one act, *Intérieur,* in which the family on which the drama bears is silent, confined between the window – through which two speakers look at it and who comment on what the family is still unaware of – and the door, through which these speakers know that the drama will be made visible to the family, in the form of the body of the girl who has thrown herself into the water. This visual structure, which is centred on silent characters, is itself the metaphor of another mutism: one by which the suicide victim took with her the reason for her act; that by which life is manifest as a confused set of reasons for living and for not living among all these anonymous beings who, just like her, are ignorant of themselves and may have said nothing until their deaths except banal things such as 'Sir, or Madam, it will rain this morning'[7] – a phrase which is the dramatic equivalent of the famous Flaubertian barometer that Barthes wanted to reduce to the self-referential function of the 'reality effect', whereas it marks the imperceptible border between life without history and the life that rushes headlong into the abyss. 'You cannot see into the soul as you see into that room', comments the old man.[8] But the visibility of the silent room, whose inhabitants do not know that misfortune awaits them, is precisely the paradoxical visibility of the soul, meaning by 'soul' all that 'surrounds' the house which likes to pretend it is sealed, the unactualizable space in which one might see develop all the ramifications through which thoughts emerge and travel, and in which the reasons each person has for speaking or for keeping quiet, for acting and for not acting are endlessly lost.

But the doors and windows of motionless theatre ordinarily take on a less literal figure. They come to appear as unforeseen openings through which fictional action is split. And the clash of wills or passions, which comprises the staple fare of plots, is opened to make way for invisible powers, which are themselves liable to divide into two: thus, in the age of Ibsen, into the determinism of heredity and into the pure chance of encounter with the Unknown. This is the logic of the split plot that I have analysed, taking Maeterlinck's lead, in Ibsen's plots and notably in *The Master Builder*.[9] In this play, we know, the social plot of the architect, who, aging, faces competition from younger individuals, and the familial plot of a marriage secretly undone, are together turned upside down by the arrival of the young Hilde, who asks Solness if, for her, he would repeat the feat that, as a child, had so awe-inspired her, and go and tie the bouquet to the peak of his latest construction: the request, a death-command for this vertigo sufferer, is one that the architect, himself a past master at cynically exploiting the talents and passions of others, will obey nonetheless, in sleepwalking, as one obeys an order from those forces of the outside that are also innermost.

The fictional logic thus splits from the inside: the calculation of ends and means is routed via an apparition that takes Solness over into true life. True life is what is manifest in images and Solness only accedes to it at the price of sacrificing everything for the mere benefit of a glorious image, one he'd left ingrained in the mind of a child. It will be said that this metaphysical solution is not yet a dramaturgical one. This child's gaze, in fact, has reality only in the words exchanged by Hilde and Solness. And words have never shown the power of a gaze. But the sensible force of theatre is made up of this very gap, of the resonance in words of their own inability to express a gaze, but also of their own ability to express the collapse of all logic of means and ends before the power of a gaze. The art of theatre consists in making resonate in words a power other than that of their meaning, the power of life as the out-place that overflows the framework of action. Now, this resonance obtains only by loosening the links that normally arrange words and the rhythm according to which they are exchanged, so that they are addressed no longer to an interlocutor but instead to the space surrounding them, and that they hollow out some presence of the invisible out-place. This, in Chekhov, is the power of those words thrown one after another like 'stones into a well', words such as those uttered by Platonov's wife, which I evoked in beginning: 'Live according to the Scriptures. The key to the chest-of-drawers is in my woollen dress' – words accompanying a suicide that soon after we learn was unsuccessful. Similarly, in *Uncle Vanya*, with Astrov's famous phrase about the heat in Africa, which is uttered in front of a map that, in this instance – as Chekhov's stage directions indicate, as though in provocation to future semiologists – clearly has no utility. Astrov's remark quite obviously conveys no particular interest for the African climate. It resonates simply to punctuate the repetitive time to which Vanya, whose crime has not taken place, and Sonia, whose love will definitively not take place, are doomed from thereon in.

The theatrical stage is thus properly the stage of thought's exceeding action. I leave aside the way in which this specificity questions worlds in which thought is presented in itself and those in which it is given as the instrument of an action. I limit myself to what this stage builds as the form and space of drama. Thought that exceeds action manifests itself there essentially as the resonance of words in a split space. A specific art is established here: staging as an art of setting words in space. This art itself tends to specialize as the art of the double plot: it builds the space of words that have to tip the explicit plot over into its sleepwalking truth. Maeterlinck performs this in thought when, in his article, he makes of the encounter between Solness and Hilde the event that clears the stage of action's lies but also of all the accessories that Ibsen meticulously describes, from glasses of water on tables up to the personages' neckties. New drama can only be written as its author's vision but, in order to realize its power of presentation of the non-present, this precise vision must be denied by the ideal space that the words outline, and even more so by the silence separating them. Gordon Craig proposed the stagecraft expression for this when he undertook to rethink Shakespearian tragedy on the basis of spectres.[10] The proper art of the theatre is to get the truth of tragedy to be seen and heard: thus, for *Macbeth*, not the story of a brave soldier corrupted by an ambitious woman, but the unfolding of a dream, a succession of visions, the hero of which suddenly awakens in the last act. The place of this dream, materialized in Craig's drawings, is a castle disproportionate in relation to any ambition for the general and a labyrinth into which Macbeth sinks as though into the darkness of the unconscious, without appearing ever able to strike the person he intends to with the knife. It is true that Craig's drawings, just like Appia's, will remain drawings. The staging that gives the plot over to its truth as waking dream will never be achieved. In embodying the new image of thought, new theatre's radicality seems doomed to exist above all in programmatic texts and sketch books.

But the construction of this space of words, which punctuates action's non-place, is only one of the two forms within which the new art of *mise-en-scène* emerges. For there is another form of the double plot, where it is the unity of the performing body that works to fill in the gap between the words of the drama and the materiality of the stage space. This form consists in embroidering onto the fictional framework of causes and effects, a scenario of pure performance. Meyerhold achieves this by reconstructing Ostrovsky's *The Forest* as a discontinuous series of episodes, each presented as the practice of a singular perfor-mance, or by transforming the mill in Crommelynck's *Le Cocu magnifique* into a springboard for a series of gymnastic exercises. A genealogy may be traced of this second form by departing from the same historical and theoretico-political moment at which the idea of popular drama emerged. The period after July 1830, when Büchner was transforming the Hugolian project of the popular theatre into the theatre of the unconscious, is also when Théophile Gautier and aesthetes among his friends were applauding Deburau's performances at the *Théâtre des Funambules*. Deburau is at once the anti-Ruy Blas and the anti-Woyzeck. He neither embodies the people claiming its place in the bright of day nor the people as the primitive expression of obscure forces. He does not embody the people at all. He carries out for it a performance that aims at nothing other than its perfect execution – which itself has no other end than the spectators' pleasure. The indissociability between an auton- omous perfection and the pleasure offered to those who taste it, such is, properly speaking, 'art for art's sake' – an expression that has remained associated with the person of the Funambules's poet spectator, the price of which has been a misinterpretation of its meaning. Art for art's sake is art that shows nothing but its performance, which does not mean that it flaunts itself or appraises itself. It is the identity between the autonomy of a self-sufficient performance and its effect in a material space of representation. This identity had until this point found its model in the coincidence between representation as the intellectually verisimilar chaining of causes and effects and representation as the performance of speaking bodies embodying characters on a stage. Well, it now finds itself cut into two. On the one hand, the intellectual chain of causes has been transformed into a theatre of visions, revoking the scenarios of verisimilitude and leaving to the dialogue between words and space the care to show, in a structurally imperfect form, the invisible process according to which visions take body. On the other hand, perfection takes refuge in the pure performance of bodies that act without repre- senting. What seems lost in this separation is the coincidence between theatre as an idea of thought's action and theatre as the idea put into action. Both ideas seem henceforth fated to gaze at each other through the window. That is what the fable of *Intérieur* symbolizes: an 'interior' that is seen only from an 'outside', on centre stage, where the characters talk about another outside, which, as for it, remains off-stage.

But the disjunction is also the principle of a supplementation. The theatre of the motionless action of thoughts and the theatre of bodies' pure performance are simultaneously the fragments of a lost body and the forms on the basis of which it is possible to supplement an 'intellectual arrangement of actions' that becomes dubious as soon as action is lost in a space unable to be circumscribed. *Mise-en-scène* as a new art emerges precisely from the separation of fictional theatrical bodies into three dissociated elements: the plot as the arrangement of actions determined by relations between characters; the theatre of thought as the play of invisible forces resonating in words that fall in the well of the stage; and the performance of bodies executed for the sake of its own perfection and for the pleasure of spectators. On occasion this art has thought of itself as the new theatrical art, built upon the ruins of the old one, and its pioneers have covered their sketchbooks with graphic compositions of this theatre-to-come. But most often art has been about combining all three elements to introduce into fictional action the decelerations specific to making fiction pass over into the truth that lies behind words or the accelerations able to project it toward its outside, whether this be the audience's pleasure or the life surrounding the theatre.

This long and complex history gets short-circuited in Barthes's trenchant judgement on the embourgeoisement of the people's theatre. He sums up the wrongdoing of the TNP's star actor in a stark opposition: Gérard Philippe *embodied* the role instead of *showing* it; he had reconstituted, on the great bare set of epic theatre, a relation of inveiglement of the audience by the actor, which was the essence of petit-bourgeois theatre. The principle of the accusation is clear. It was the time when Barthes was to discover Brecht and the severity of the opposition between the bourgeois theatre of identification and the proletarian theatre of estrangement (*Verfremdung*) which gives the spectator, along with the freedom to judge, the weapon of knowledge, which is the condition of action. But the simple opposition between identification and estrangement had, for Brecht, been a way of liquidating the long period of experimentation during which theatre in times of proletarian revolution had sought to bring closer to direct political action a theatrical heritage that was torn between the stage of dream-thoughts and the platform of gymnastic performances. From his Danish exile, Brecht was to resolve against forms of expressionist theatre as well as of theatrical activism: these forms may have been able to maximize the spectators' pleasure, but it taught them nothing about how to perform on the stage of political action.[11] In order to tie together again instruction and pleasure, it was necessary to choose between a theatre of identification, which hypnotizes spectators, and a theatre of estrangement, which offers them weapons of critique. This meant forgetting that the supposed theatre of identification was an internally divided theatre, one that already bore its own effects of estrangement, effects tied to the tensions between several plots and several manners of feeling its effect. It also meant forgetting that at the heart of these tensions, a chasm had been hollowed out via a logic that sought to think theatre's action from within a simple relation between four terms, by having passivity rhyme with illusion and resolute action with clear knowledge. Now, this logic, which entered into crisis in the times of Rousseau and Schiller, is the one that Barthes, following Brecht, meant to reaffirm. That is what he recapitulated in the amazing syllogism formulated in his text on 'Mother Courage Blind': 'Because we *see* Mother Courage blind, we *see* what she doesn't',[12] an argument that is itself built on a game of hide-and-seek. For, in order to admit the improbable deduction according to which seeing the blind brings lucidity, it is necessary already to have admitted that the blind person is blind, that Mother Courage losing her children is the victim of her blindness. Now, Brecht's play shows that Mother Courage is perfectly clear-sighted and that the loss of her children counts for her among the collateral damage that all commerce entails. The history of Catherine's death or of Schweizerkas's, then, has a moral no different from that borne by the noise of small Hedwige's gunshot in the attic of *The Wild Duck*: a story about how parents sacrifice their children for the interests of their commerce or the satisfaction of their own image.

To explain these crimes, Brecht certainly has a more convincing explanation of the world and one bearing more hopes than Ibsen's 'vital lie'. But the problem is to grasp the link that is established between this knowledge and the performance presented on the stage. It is to grasp how it is possible to go not from Mother Courage's ignorance to Marxist knowledge but instead from the knowledge that Mother Courage and Marxism jointly possess about the spoils of war into action to bring about a world where what are saved are not profits but children. This question acquired some insistence when the play was being written, that is to say, when the homeland of communism allied with Hitlerian Germany through that well-known pact. At this very time the beautiful logic relating Mother Courage's acts to their final social cause had to include, with the memory of Hedwige's pistol shot, the question on which Büchner, Ibsen, Chekhov and others showed the entire efficacy of knowledge to depend. That question, by which politics is tied to the theatre, is not to know how to exit the dream in order to act in real life. It is to decide what is dream and what is true life.

ORIGIN OF TEXTS

Work on the reality effect first began with Maria Mühle's invitation to the Bauhaus-Universität in Weimar in June 2009. A first written version appeared in German in the framework of the collective volume *Realismus in den Künsten der Gegenwart* edited by D. Linck, M. Lüthy, B. Obermayr and M. Vöhler (Diaphanes, 2010).

The work on Virginia Woolf originated with the colloquium 'Virginia Woolf parmi les philosophes', organized by Chantal Delourme and Richard Pédot and held at the Collège international de philosophie in March 2012. The colloquium's proceedings were published on the online journal *Le Tour critique* (2013, vol. II). Another version was presented at the colloquium of the Society for Novel Studies, organized by Nancy Armstrong in Durham in April 2012, and was published in *Novel*, vol. XLVII, no. 2, summer 2014.

A first version of 'Spider's Work' was published in *Studies in Romanticism*, vol. L, no. 2, Summer 2011, at the invitation of Emily Rohrbach and Emily Sun.

'The Infinite Taste of the Republic' was written for the special issue *Time for Baudelaire (Poetry, Theory, History)* edited by

E. S. Burt, Elissa Marder and Kevin Newmark, *Yale French Studies*, vol. CXXV, Spring 2014.

A first version of 'The Theatre of Thought' was presented at the colloquium 'Image et fonctions du théâtre dans la philosophie française contemporaine', held at the École normale supérieure in October–November 2012, at the initiative of Flore Garcin-Marrou and Dimitra Panopoulos.

The reflections on the politics of fiction were put forward, in diverse versions, at the universities of Madison, Atlanta, Berne, Rabat, Toronto and Trent, as well as at the Facultad Libre de Rosario, at the Academia de Humanismo Cristiano in Santiago and at the European Graduate School. I thank all those who invited me and joined in discussing my propositions.

NOTES

Translator's Introduction

1 See, Fredric Jameson, *The Antinomies of Realism,* London: Verso, 2013, p. 6.

2 Ibid., p. 5.

Foreword

1 Barbey d'Aurevilly, 'Gustave Flaubert', in *Les Hommes et les oeuvres. Le Roman contemporain,* Slatkine reprints, 1968, vol. XVIII, p. 103, and 'From Captain Conrad's *Lord Jim*', *The Queen, The Lady's Newspaper,* 3 Nov. 1900, in Allan H. Simmons (ed.) *Joseph Conrad, Contemporary Reviews,* Vol. 1. Cambridge: Cambridge University Press, 2012, p. 293.

2 Flaubert, letter to Louis Bouilhet, 8 December 1853, *Correspondance,* Paris: Gallimard, Bibliothèque de la Pléiade, 1980, vol. II, p. 472.

3 Conrad, letter to William Hugh Clifford, 13 December 1899, *The Collected Letters of Joseph Conrad,* edited by Frederick R. Karl and Laurence Davies, Cambridge University Press, 1986, vol. 2, p. 226.

4 On the problem of *Lord Jim's* ending see the letter to William Blackwood dated 19 July 1900, in *The Collected Letters of Joseph Conrad,* vol. 2, p. 283.

5   Translator's note – *Fait divers* is often rendered as 'news item' or even 'minor news item' in English, but I've chosen to retain the French term since what it relays is more than just something of secondary importance (e.g. a run-over dog). A *fait divers* is a type of event that is properly unclassifiable in any of the rubrics that make up current affairs (national, international, political, economic, and so on) and that have a more general bearing. The *fait divers* is rather an accident in the social order, often unfortunate, and is unlinked either to current affairs or to other *faits divers.*

Madame Aubain's barometer

1   Gustav Flaubert, 'A Simple Heart', in *Three Tales,* translated and with an Introduction by A. J. Krailsheimer, Oxford: Oxford World's Classics, 1999, p. 3. (French original, 1877.)

2   André Breton, 'Manifesto of Surrealism', in *Manifestoes of Surrealism*, translated by Richard Seaver and Helen R. Lane, University of Michigan Press: Ann Arbor, 1969, p. 7. (French original, 1924.)

3   Jorge Luis Borges, Prologue to Adolfo Bioy Casares, *The Invention of Morel,* trans. Ruth L. C. Simms, New York: New York Review Books, 2003, p. 40. (Spanish original, 1940.)

4   Roland Barthes, 'The Reality Effect', *The Rustle of Language*, trans. Richard Howard, Berkeley: University of California Press, 1989, p. 141. (French original, *Le Bruissement de la langue,* 1993.)

5   Ibid., p. 147.

6   Barbey d'Aurevilly, 'Gustave Flaubert' in *Les Hommes et les OEuvres. Le Roman contemporain*, p. 103. (my translation – SC.)

7   Aristotle, *Poetics,* 1451 b7.

8   Armand de Pontmartin, *Nouvelles causeries du samedi,* 1860, pp. 321–2.

9   Charlotte Brontë, *Jane Eyre,* Penguin Classics, 2006, p. 129.

10   See 'Plebeian Heaven' in Jacques Rancière, *Aisthesis: Scenes of the aesthetic regime of art*, translated by Zakir Paul, London: Verso, 2011, pp. 39–53. (French original, 2011.)

11   Gustav Flaubert, *Madame Bovary*, translated and with an Introduction and Notes by Lydia Davis, London: Penguin Classics, 2010, part 1, Ch. 9. (French original, 1856.)

Marlow's lie

1   Virginia Woolf, 'Modern Fiction', in *The Common Reader, The Essays of Virginia Woolf*, edited by Andrew McNeillie, Hogarth Press, 1994, vol. IV, 1925–8, pp. 157–65.

2   Ibid., p. 160.

3   Ibid.

4   Ibid.

5   Virginia Woolf, 'The Mark on the Wall', in *The Mark on the Wall and Other Short Fiction*, Oxford: Oxford University Press, 2008, p. 8.

6   Woolf, 'Modern Fiction', p. 160.

7   Joseph Conrad, *Heart of Darkness*, London: Penguin Books, p. 6.

8   Letter to R. B. Cunningham Graham, 14 January 1898, in *The Collected Letters of Joseph Conrad*, eds Frederick R. Karl and Laurence Davies, Cambridge: Cambridge University Press, vol. 2, 1898–1902, p. 17.

9   Joseph Conrad, *The Portable Conrad*, edited and with an Introduction by Michael Gorra, London: Penguin Classics, p. 48.

10   Ibid., p. 47.

11   Letter to John Galsworthy, 11 November 1901, in *The Collected Letters of Joseph Conrad*, vol. 2, p. 359.

12   Letter to Hugh Clifford, 9 October 1999, ibid., p. 200.

13   Letter to T. Fisher Unwin, 22 August 1896, vol. 1, ibid, pp. 302–3.

14   Conrad, *Lord Jim: A Tale,* Oxford: Oxford World's Classics, 2008, pp. 21–2.

15   Ibid., p. 57.

16   Conrad, *Nostromo*, Oxford: Oxford World's Classics, 2007, p. 48.

17   Ibid., p. 79.

18   Conrad, *Lord Jim*, p. 163.

19   Ibid.

20   Conrad, *Heart of Darkness,* p. 94.

21   Ibid., p. 148.

The death of Prue Ramsay

1   Virginia Woolf, 'To the Lighthouse,' in *Selected Works of Virginia Woolf*, Hertfordshire: Wordsworth Editions, 2007, p. 282.

2   Ibid., p. 341.

3   Ibid., p. 341.

4   Ibid., p. 342.

5   Virginia Woolf, *The Waves,* Oxford: Oxford World's Classics, 2015, p. 28.

6   Ibid., p. 40.

7   Woolf, *Mrs. Dalloway,* Oxford: Oxford World's Classics, 2008, pp. 157–8.

8   Ibid., 156.

9   Ibid., p. 71.

10   Ibid., p. 72.

11   James Agee, *Let Us Now Praise Famous Men*, Mariner Books, 2001 (Original, 1941), pp. 225–7.

12   Ibid., p. 146.

13   Ibid., p. 267.

14   Ibid., p. 309.

Spider's work

1   Cf. Nicholas Roe, 'Keats's Commonwealth', in *Keats and History,*
     Cambridge: Cambridge University Press, 1995, pp. 194–211, and *Keats
     and the Culture of Dissent,* Oxford: Clarendon Press, 1997, pp. 257–67.

2   Hazlitt, *Lectures of The English Poets,* in *The Selected Writings of
     William Hazlitt,* ed. Duncan Wu, London: Pickering and Chatto,
     1998, vol. 2, pp. 165–6.

3   Letter to J. H. Reynolds, 19 February 1818, in John Keats, *The
     Letters of John Keats* 1814–1821, ed. Hyder Edward Rollins, vol. 1,
     Cambridge: Cambridge University Press, 1958, p. 231.

4   William Hazlitt, *Lectures on the English Poets,* p. 166.

5   Letter to his brothers, 21 December 1817, in John Keats, *The Letters
     of John Keats*, *op. cit.* p. 193

6   'We hate poetry that has a palpable design upon us—and if we do
     not agree, seems to put its hand in its breeches pocket'. Letter to
     J. H. Reynolds, 3 February 1818, vol. 1, p. 224. Wordsworth is the
     target here.

7   Friedrich Schiller, *Letters on the Aesthetic Education of Man*, ed.
     and trans. Elizabeth M. Wilkinson and L. A. Willoughby, Oxford:
     Clarendon Press, 1982, p. 157. (translation modified – SC.)

8   John Keats, 'Endymion', in *John Keats,* ed. Elizabeth Cook, Oxford:
     Oxford University Press, 1994, p. 59, lines 880–7.

9   Ibid., p. 57, lines 788–90.

10   Keats, 'The Fall of Hyperion: A Dream', in *John Keats,* ed.
     Elizabeth Cook, Oxford: Oxford University Press, 1994, p. 184, lines
     199–202.

11   'Ode to Indolence', in *John Keats*, p. 173.

12   William Wordsworth, *The Excursion*, London: Edward Moxon, 1847, pp. 322–4.

13   Ibid., p. 315, line 3.

14   Ibid., p. 326, lines 326/27.

15   Hazlitt, *Lectures on The English Poets,* in *The Selected Writings of William Hazlitt,* vol. II, p. 316 and 'Observations on Mr Wordsworth's Poem the *Excursion,* The Round Table' in *The Selected Writings*, vol. II, p. 112–20.

16   Keats, 'Letter to Mrs James Wylie, 6 August, 1818', in *Letters of John Keats,* p. 360.

17   Keats, *John Keats,* p. 176.

18   See Jacques Rancière, *The Ignorant Schoolmaster: Five Lessons in Intellectual Emancipation*, translated, with an Introduction, by Kristin Ross, Stanford CA: Stanford University Press, 1991.

19   Keats, 'The Fall of Hyperion', in *John Keats,* p. 180.

20   Kant, *Critique of Judgement,* trans. Paul Guyer and Eric Matthews, Cambridge: Cambridge University Press, p. 229. (German original: *Kritik der Urteilskraft*, 1790.)

21   Keats, 'Letter to Reynolds from 19 February 1818,' *Letters of John Keats*, p. 232.

22   Flaubert, Letter to Louise Colet, 26–7 May 1853, *Correspondance,* Paris: Gallimard, Bibliothèque de la Pléiade, 1980, vol. II, p. 335. (my translation – SC.)

The infinite taste of the republic

1   Charles Baudelaire, 'Pierre Dupont' in *Œuvres complètes*, ed. Claude Pichois, Gallimard, Bibliothèque de la Pléiade, 1976, vol. 2, p. 34.

2   Baudelaire, 'The Exposition Universelle' *Art in Paris 1845–1862*, ed.

and trans. Jonathan Mayne, Ithaca: Cornell University Press, 1981, 123. (French original, *Exposition universelle de 1855*.)

3   Ibid., p. 123.

4   Baudelaire, 'The Painter of Modern Life', *The Painter of Modern Life and Other Essays,* trans. Jonathan Mayne, London: Phaidon Press, 1964, p. 10. (French original, 'Le peintre de la vie moderne,' 1863.)

5   Baudelaire 'The Salon of 1859', *Art in Paris 1845–1862,* p. 149.

6   Ibid., p. 200. (translation modified – SC.)

7   Walter Benjamin, 'The Paris of the Second Empire in Baudelaire', in *The Writer of Modern Life,* ed. Michel Jennings, trans. Howard Eiland, Edmund Jephcott, Rodney Livingston and Harry Zohn, Cambridge, MA and London: The Belknap Press of Harvard University Press, 2006, pp. 85, 88. (translation modified – SC.)

8   Baudelaire, 'Further Notes on Edgar Poe', *The Painter of Modern Life,* p. 99.

9   Ibid.

10   Baudelaire, 'The Salon of 1859', p. 185.

11   Baudelaire, 'St. Peter's Denial,' *The Flowers of Evil* trans. James McGowan, Oxford: Oxford University Press, 1993, p. 265. (translation modified – SC.) (French original, 'Le reniement de saint Pierre', *Les Fleurs du mal*, 1857.)

12   Barbey d'Aurevilly, 'Flaubert, L'Education sentimentale', *Le Roman contemporain. Les Œuvres et les Hommes,* p. 101. (Barbey's emphasis.)

13   Baudelaire, 'Edgar Poe', p. 105. (French original, 1856.)

14   Baudelaire, 'On Wine and Hashish', Foreword by Margaret Drabble, trans. Andrew Brown, London: Hesperus Press, 2002. (French original, *Du vin et du haschisch*, 1851.)

15   Baudelaire, 'Some Foreign Caricaturists', *The Painter of Modern Life,* p. 196.

16   Baudelaire, 'Letter to Armand Fraisse of 18 February 1860', *Correspondance*, ed. Claude Pichois and Jean Ziegler, Paris: Gallimard, Bibliothèque de la Pléiade, 1973, vol. I, p. 676.

17 Baudelaire, 'The Salon of 1846', p. 75. (translation modified – SC.)

18 Honoré de Balzac, *Ferragus*: *Chief of the Devorants,* trans. Katharine Prescott Wormeley, New York: Silver Scroll Publishing, 2015.

19 Baudelaire, 'The Salon of 1846', pp. 118–19.

20 Ibid., p. 59.

21 Baudelaire, 'To a Woman Passing By', *The Flowers of Evil,* p. 189. (French original, 'À une passante', *Les Fleurs du mal,* 1957.)

22 Baudelaire, 'Windows', *Paris Spleen,* p. 76. (French original, 'Les Fenetres', *Spleen de Paris,* 1855.) (translation modified – SC.)

23 Honoré de Balzac, *The Wild Skin's Ass,* trans. Helen Constantine, Oxford: Oxford University Press, 2012, p. 75. (translation modified – SC.) (French original, 1831.)

24 Victor Hugo, 'The Slope of Reverie', in *Selected Poems of Victor Hugo: A Bilingual Edition,* trans. E. H. and A. M. Blackmore, Chicago: University of Chicago Press, 2001, p. 41.

25 Baudelaire, 'A Carcass', *The Flowers of Evil,* pp. 59–63. (French original, 'Une charogne', *Les Fleurs du mal,* 1857.)

26 Baudelaire, 'The Windows', *Paris Spleen,* p. 76.

27 Baudelaire, 'The Old Acrobat', *Paris Spleen,* pp. 27–8.

28 Ibid., p. 28.

29 Baudelaire, 'The Eyes of the Poor', *Paris Spleen,* p. 53. (translation modified – SC.)

30 Baudelaire, 'Crowds', *Paris Spleen,* p. 23. (translation modified – SC.)

The theatre of thoughts

1   Anton Chekhov, *Platonov*. (My emphasis. I provide this passage here, such as I heard it, in Pol Quentin's translation used for the portrayal of the TNP: *Ce fou de Platonov*, L'Arche, 1956, p. 79.) [Translator's note – An English translation, which differs from the one Rancière cites in being closer to the original Russian, can be found in 'Platonov', in *Twelve Plays,* Oxford World's Classics, translated and with an Introduction and Notes by Ronald Hingley, Oxford: Oxford University Press, 1992, p. 357.]

2   Roland Barthes, 'Fin de *Richard II'*, in *Écrits sur le théâtre*, ed. Jean-Loup Rivière, Points/Seuil, 2002, pp. 62–7.

3   Victor Hugo, Preface to *Marie Tudor*, in *Théâtre*, Gallimard, Bibliothèque de la Pléiade, 1964, vol. II, p. 414.

4   Georg Büchner, *Danton's Death,* in a new version by Howard Brenton from literal translations by Jane Fry and Simon Scardifield, London: Methuen Drama, 2010, p. 9. (translation modified – SC.) (German original, 1835.)

5   Ibid., p. 22.

6   On these insurrectional republican attempts, which form the backdrop against which Büchner develops his critical reflection, the reader ought to read the astonishing documents collected by Frédéric Metz in *Georg Büchner, biographie générale*, Rennes: Editions Pontcerq, 2012.

7   Maurice Maeterlinck, 'Interior,' in *Modern Short Plays,* ed. Leslie Rees, Sydney: Angus and Robertson, 1967, p. 68. (French original, 1999.)

8   Ibid., p. 69.

9   Rancière, *Aisthesis.* pp. 111–31.

10 Edward Gordon Craig, 'On the ghosts in the tragedies of Shakespeare' in *On the Art of the Theatre*, Heinemann, 1956, pp. 264–80. See also, 'The Temple Staircase' in Rancière, *Aisthesis*, pp. 171–90.

11   Bertolt Brecht, 'On experimental theatre', in *Brecht on Theatre*, eds
     Marc Silberman, Steve Giles and Tom Kuhn. London: Bloomsbury
     Methuen Drama, pp. 133–46.

12   Barthes, 'Mother Courage Blind', in *Critical Essays,* trans. Richard
     Howard, Evanston: Northwestern University Press, p. 34 (Barthes'
     emphasis). We find a similar argument applied by Barthes to the
     figure of Charlot in 'The Poor and the Proletarian', *Mythologies,*
     trans. Annette Lavers, London: Vintage, 2000, p. 39. (French
     original, 1970.)

INDEX